Multiscale Spectral–Spatial Feature Learning for Hyperspectral Image Classification

Newton

Contents

1 Introduction **1**

1.1 Hyperspectral Imagery 2

1.1.1 Pixel-wise classification of HSI 5

1.1.2 Challenges in classification of HSI 7

1.1.2.1 High dimensionality of HSI 7

1.1.2.2 High intraclass variability and low interclass variability 8

1.1.2.3 Incorporating spatial information 8

1.1.2.4 Limited labelled samples 9

1.1.2.5 Curse of dimensionality 9

1.2 Background Literature 10

1.2.1 Dimensionality reduction 11

1.2.1.1 Feature Selection 11

1.2.1.2 Feature Extraction 12

1.2.2 Incorporation of spatial information for analysis of HSI . . . 15

1.2.3 Active learning for hyperspectral image classification 25

1.2.4 Sparse Representation Classification for the analysis of HSI . 32

1.3 Objectives 38

1.4 Organization of the thesis 40

2 Component Adaptive Sparse Representation for Hyperspectral Image Classification **43**

2.1 Introduction 43

2.2 Proposed Method 45

2.2.1 Proposed Attribute Filtering 46
2.2.2 Component Adaptive Multiscale Windows 50
2.2.3 Component Adaptive Sparse Representation Classification (CASRC) 52
2.3 Experimental Results 54
2.3.1 Experimental Setup 54
2.3.2 Results 55
2.3.3 Discussion 64
2.4 Conclusion 65

3 Dictionary Learning using Novel Multiscale Context Sensitive Spectral Features for Classification of Hyperspectral Imagery 67

3.1 Introduction 67
3.2 Background 70
3.2.1 Singular Value Decomposition (SVD) 70
3.2.2 Discriminative K-SVD (DKSVD) 71
3.3 Proposed Technique 72
3.3.1 Identification of the appropriate neighbourhood of the pixels 73
3.3.2 Extraction of context-sensitive spectral features (CSSF) . . . 74
3.3.3 Generation of multiscale CSSF 74
3.3.4 Learning dictionaries using DKSVD 76
3.3.5 Classification of HSI 76
3.4 Experimental Results 77
3.4.1 Experimental Setup 78
3.4.2 Results 79
3.4.2.1 Results: Indian Pines 79
3.4.2.2 Results: Pavia University 81
3.4.2.3 Results: University of Houston 2013 82
3.4.3 Ablation Analysis 84
3.4.4 Computational Time 86
3.4.5 Discussion 87

3.5 Conclusion 88

4 Multiscale rank-1 spectral spatial features for hyperspectral image classification 90

4.1 Introduction 90

4.2 Proposed Method 92

4.2.1 Extraction of rank-1 spectral-spatial features (RSSF) 93

4.2.2 Generation of multiscale RSSF (MRSSF) 94

4.2.3 Classification of HSI 95

4.3 Experimental Results 97

4.3.1 Experimental Setup 97

4.3.2 Results 98

4.4 Conclusion 109

5 Active Learning for Hyperspectral Image Classification Using Kernel Sparse Representation Classifiers 111

5.1 Introduction 111

5.2 Sparse representation classifiers in kernel space 113

5.2.1 Kernel Sparse Representation Classification (KSRC) 114

5.2.2 Multifeature Kernel Sparse Representation Classification . . 115

5.3 Proposed Method 116

5.3.1 Proposed KBT-DCBD 116

5.3.1.1 Proposed Kernel Breaking Tie 116

5.3.1.2 Proposed Dictionary Correlation Based Diversity . 117

5.3.2 Proposed MKBT-MDCBD 120

5.3.2.1 Proposed Multifeature Kernel Breaking Tie 120

5.3.2.2 Proposed Multifeature Dictionary Correlation Based Diversity 121

5.4 Experimental Results 123

5.4.1 Design of Experiments 123

5.4.2 Results 124

5.5 Conclusion 128

6 Conclusion and future direction 130

6.1 Contribution 1 : A component adaptive sparse representation classification 130

6.1.1 Limitations and future works 131

6.2 Contribution 2: A novel dictionary learning method for HSI Classification 131

6.2.1 Limitations and future works 132

6.3 Contribution 3: A novel spectral-spatial feature set for HSI classification 132

6.3.1 Limitations and future works 133

6.4 Contribution 4: Active learning criteria by exploiting KSRC 133

6.4.1 Limitations and future works 134

Chapter 1

Introduction

Information gathered from a distance is called remote sensing. In terms of earth observation, this refers to using sensors to gather visual data about the geographical features of the planet. These sensors can be divided into many categories. They can be either airborne based or spaceborne based depending on their height, and depending on their mode of operations they can be either active or passive. Active sensors emit their own light, whereas passive sensors used the reflected light of the sun to measure the intensity of objects. Of the two, the passive sensors are the ones used for taking the HSI of the earth's geographical areas. They accomplish this by capturing different wavelengths of the electromagnetic spectrum and storing them contiguously into hundreds of bands to form an image cube. As a result, HSI provides extensive spectral information that has aided in the development of numerous applications, such as earth monitoring, quality assessment of resources, object identification and extraction, classification etc [3, 37, 154]. Among these, the classification task still remains a challenge to this day due to various constraints, such as the large volume of data, the inherent noise of HSI, and the limited availability of labelled samples [151]. In this thesis, some advanced sparse representation techniques that exploit spatial and spectral information are proposed.

This chapter presents the overview of the thesis. First, the basics of HSI classification and its various challenges are presented. Then a detailed background literature in the context of this research are reviewed, followed by the objectives

Table 1.1: Some well known hyperspectral sensors with their specifications

Sensor	Spectral bands	Spectral resolution	Spectral range	Spatial resolution	Platform used
AISAEagle	488	3.3nm	400-970nm	0.52m	Airborne
AVIRIS-NG	600	5nm	380-2510nm	0.3-0.4nm	Airborne
AVIRIS	224	10nm	400-2500nm	30m	Airborne
CASI	144	2.4nm	360-1050nm	2.5m	Airborne
EnMAP	228	5.25-12.5nm	420-2400nm	30m	Spaceborne
HYDICE	210	10.2nm	400-2500nm	1-7m	Airborne
HYPERION	220	10nm	400-2500nm	30m	Spaceborne
HypXIM	210	10nm	400-2500nm	8m	Spaceborne
ROSIS	115	4nm	430-830nm	1.3m	Airborne
TianGong-1	128	10-23nm	400-2500nm	10-20m	Spaceborne

and the contribution of this research. Lastly, the organization of this thesis is given in a point by point manner.

1.1 Hyperspectral Imagery

Hyperspectral imaging is the process of obtaining the spectral information of a given geographic area by means of imaging spectrometers, sometimes referred to as hyperspectral sensors. There are a wide variety of sensors with different specifications and capabilities, as shown in Table 1.1 [12, 72]. And unlike other sensors, such as multispectral and color(RGB) sensors, these hyperspectral sensors are powerful and cover the spectral information contiguously across different wavelength, permitting the creation of spectral signatures for different objects. The result of this is an HSI where each pixel represents unique spectral signatures. In greater detail, the HSI consists of multiple stacked grayscale images, where each individual grayscale image represents a specific spectral band, forming a three-dimensional spectral cube. This image has two spatial dimensions and one spectral dimension which are derived from the satellite swath widths across-track, along-track, and wavelength range respectively. The smallest unit in the image is a 1-D vector called a pixel, and it holds a unique spectrum of an area whose size depends on the spatial resolution of the sensor. Figure 1-1 show the representation of hyperspectral data. Figure 1-1a shows a single spectral band of HSI represented as a gray-scale image, while Figure 1-1b shows how these bands are stacked together to form the 3-D cube HSI. Finally, Figure 1-1c shows the variation of the pixel's intensities across different spectral bands, also called the spectral signature of the pixel. Now, these spectral signatures are different for every object or surface material, and hence they can be used to identify and quantify their presence in the scene.

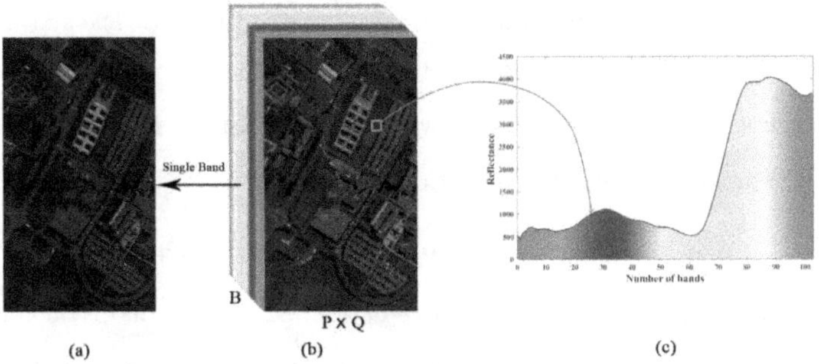

Figure 1-1: Illustration of the HSI framework, a) single band grayscale image, b) Hyperspectral image, c) Reflectance values of single pixel.

Hyperspectral imaging has become increasingly popular due to the non-invasive, and non-destructive capability in identifying and quantifying materials. Further, the resultant HSI has rich spectral information, which has proved vital for various industries and research applications. A few of these applications are detailed below.

- Agriculture: The high spectral resolution of HSI have proven to be valuable in agriculture, particularly in the domains of vegetation analysis and precision farming. It offers a wide range of applications such as plant disease estimation, wetland mapping and precise crop classification [48, 62, 92, 152, 251].
- Mineral Exploration: The availability of HSI has offered a minimally invasive and cost-effective approach for performing multiple tasks such as sustainable exploration, mapping and identification of minerals [13, 48, 114].
- Environmental Monitoring: HSI has also become widely popular for tracking changes in the environmental conditions and the impacts of current and

future human activities. Many applications such as characterization of surface materials, urban area mapping, pollution detection and water quality assessment were made possible by exploiting the HSI [81, 146, 186, 209].

- Disaster Management: Proper planning and decision-making is a must to minimize the costs of natural and man-induced disaster. The arrival of HSI has opened up to a wide variety of applications to meet these demands such as accurate monitoring of wildfires, post-disaster forensics, earthquake forecasting and landslide detection [111, 203, 244, 257].

- Water Resource Management: Water resources are a vital part of the ecosystem, serving as a natural resource as well as a social and economic asset. Many aspects of water resource management have benefited from hyperspectral imagery. Some of the applications used are mapping of the small water bodies, water quality assessment and sediment analysis [23, 70, 174].

- Forest Management: Forest management plays a vital role in ensuring a sustainable environment on earth. The HSI has been extensively used in various applications, including tree species classification, forest regeneration, and forest mapping, to support these efforts. [130, 147, 217, 228].

- Military : Collecting airborne and spaceborne intelligence, surveillance, and reconnaissance (ISR) information is mandatory for addressing the defense challenges posed in the 21st century. And HSI is a key tool for this as it offers a wide variety of applications such as distinguishing hidden features and camouflage, identifying chemical agents in plumes, tagging disturbed earth over buried objects and image classification [112, 194, 215].

As observed, the HSI has many benefits that lead to its usage in a wide variety of applications. But, each of them was tackled with different analysis and processing approaches that exploited the characteristics of HSI. Some of these approaches are image enhancement [55, 116, 140, 231], denoising [134, 193, 218], object detection [139, 170, 248], segmentation [7, 182, 204, 272], texture analysis [59, 270, 274], spectral unmixing [51, 98], and pixel-wise classification [8, 69, 201, 249, 261]. Among these approaches, pixel-wise image classification is one among the most popular approaches, since it is an important tool for a wide variety of applications. Although several methods exist in the literature for this purpose, there are still many challenges that exist today.This thesis emphasizes pixel-wise classification and the development of advanced methods to tackle its associated challenges. The subsequent subsection will discuss HSI pixel-wise classification and its associated key challenges in detail.

1.1.1 Pixel-wise classification of HSI

Pixel-wise classification of HSI follows the same fundamental principle as that applied to other types of images, such as RGB or multispectral data. Specifically, it involves the assignment of a class label to each individual pixel within the HSI [122, 235]. This process can be carried out in two ways: unsupervised and supervised [150, 269]. The unsupervised approach is quite straightforward, as it simply cluster the image pixels together based on a similarity measure. Here, no labelled samples are required by the model. On the other hand, the supervised approach requires labelled samples in order to classify the images.

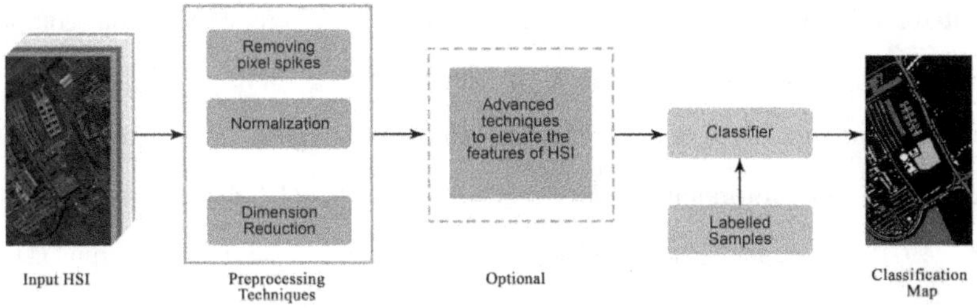

Figure 1-2: Stages of HSI Classification

In supervised pixel-wise classification of HSI, there are three primary elements that are involved; the input image, labelled (training) samples, and classifier. The input image is the hyperspectral dataset that is presented as a cube such that each pixel is a spectral vector. The labelled (training) samples are the pixels in the image that have been assigned a class based on the photo interpretation by the expert or through field survey. And the classifier is an algorithm that categorized the objects in the image into different sets of classes. So, considering these three elements, pixel-wise classification of HSI can be defined as the process of categorizing unknown pixels in the image into different classes by a classifier using the labelled pixels that have been collected. The breakdown of the classification of the HSI into stages is shown in Figure 1-2. First, the input HSI is cleaned up in a pre-processing step. This might involve removing pixel spikes, normalizing the values, and reducing the dimensions. This makes the data more accurate and easier to analyse by reducing the errors, and also to avoid the *curse of dimensionality.* After this clean-up, there's an optional stage where some advanced techniques can be used to refine the image even further. These techniques will elevate the important features in the image, making them more discriminative and more accurate in their representation. This additional step may result in better classification performance. Finally, in the last stage, with the help of labelled samples, the image is classified using a classifier. The output of this process is a classification or thematic map of different types of classes.

Selecting the right classifier for pixelwise hyperspectral classification is crucial as it directly affects the experimental outcome, like accuracy, precision, computation time, or any other analysis. In the literature, there are different types of classifiers such as support vector machine (SVM) [135, 238], random forest (RF) [138, 216], multinomial logistic regression (MLR) [237], neural network (NN) [196, 197], sparse representation classifiers (SRC) [168, 263] and deep learning (DL) [80, 141]. Among these, the SRC have demonstrated their robustness in pixelwise classification of HSI, and it offers certain advantages over other classifiers. Firstly, the SRC is a lazy learner, which means that unlike the classifiers mentioned above, it does not require training of the labelled samples. Secondly, it is not affected when labelled samples are removed, unlike other classifiers which require retraining of the model. Thirdly, it requires less processing power and offers better interpretability, unlike deep learning models. Finally, it can also seamlessly incorporate spatial information, unlike the SVM or RF model. Therefore, this thesis presents robust advanced sparse representation techniques for the classification of HSIs.

1.1.2 Challenges in classification of HSI

Although the HSI has a wealth of information, extracting this information for classification can be difficult due to many challenges. One major challenge is the high dimensionality of HSI, which interrupts its analysis and processing. Another challenge is the high intraclass and low interclass variability, caused by several factors such as low resolution, the presence of noisy bands due to instrumental error, and the high correlation among the bands in HSI. In addition, HSI also has a limited availability of labelled samples. This limitation, coupled with its high dimensionality, gives rise to the *curse of dimensionality* also known as *Hughes phenomenon*, which consequently amplifies estimation errors in classification tasks. So, one way to mitigate these problems is to use dimensional reduction techniques. This will help to eliminate redundancy in the data and keep only the important features. Then, to improve classification accuracy, proper spatial information can be incorporated into the model along with spectral information. Furthermore, active learning can be implemented to overcome the challenge faced due to the limited availability of labelled samples. However, while these concepts will mitigate the above challenges, developing methods that effectively utilize them for efficient HSI classification remains an ongoing challenge. The following subsections will describe these challenges in detail.

1.1.2.1 High dimensionality of HSI

The HSI can capture hundreds of bands of different wavelengths, spanning continuously across them. And therefore, each pixel in the image is a spectrum represented by a long vector with numerous elements. This high dimensionality increases the data storage and computation costs. Further, it is found that the high-dimensional data space of HSI is also almost empty. This makes it difficult for many analysis and processing, leading to an increase in estimation errors and deteriorate the performance of the classifier [45, 54]. One solution to this is to lower the dimension of the HSI data without losing important information.

1.1.2.2 High intraclass variability and low interclass variability

Distinguishing different materials in HSI is difficult due to high intraclass variability and low interclass variability. Intraclass variability refers to the amount of variations within classes in the dataset, whereas interclass variability refers to the amount of variations between the classes in the dataset. In HSI, this is caused due to the changes in environmental conditions, presence of clouds, slight variations in pure materials or illumination conditions and uncontrollable changes in the reflectance captured by the HSI sensor. It is also caused by the fact that, the HSI pixels often cover large spatial regions of the earth's surface with low/medium spatial resolution, thereby generating mixed spectral signatures. The combination of these two types of variability makes it difficult for image classification algorithms to accurately distinguish between different materials in HSI data [159, 275]. This is why achieving high classification accuracy remains a challenge in this field.

1.1.2.3 Incorporating spatial information

Pixel-level classification methods mainly exploit discriminant spectral information in HSI to distinguish varying objects in the scene. However, due to the existence of noise and mixed spectral pixels in HSI as mentioned above, the pixel-level methods are likely to generate noisy appearance in classification maps. But in HSI, objects in the scene are usually homogeneous in nature, which means that spatially neighbouring pixels are usually of the same class. This spatial contextual information act as complementary information to the spectral information, which help in reducing labelling uncertainties between classes having similar spectral responses. Further, it also helps in mitigating the effects of noisy pixel, potentially improving the classification accuracy [113, 166]. However, this fusion of spectral and spatial information is still a challenging task till today.

1.1.2.4 Limited labelled samples

Supervised classifiers require large number of labelled samples for accurate classification of HSI. However, experts have revealed that the ratio of unlabelled samples to labelled samples is quite large when it comes to HSI data. This is mainly because, in remote sensing, data annotation is a difficult and expensive task. It first requires the removal of noise caused by the instrument's inaccuracy or atmospheric interference, and then the pixels need to be validated either through field survey or photo interpretation by experts [207, 232]. As a consequence, the HSI classification will face an underfitting or overfitting problem and, with the high dimensionality of HSI, may also lead to the *curse of dimensionality.*

1.1.2.5 Curse of dimensionality

The phenomenon known as the *curse of dimensionality* or the *Hughes effect* describes the observation that for a constant number of training samples, increasing the dimensionality of the feature initially improves the classification accuracy by providing more discriminative information. However, beyond a certain threshold, a further increase will subsequently cause a decrease in accuracy. This occurs because the classifier becomes overwhelmed by the high dimensionality and the limited amount of training data, resulting in overfitting and reduced generalization capability [93, 181]. To enhance the generalization of the model, it is often necessary to acquire more training data. However, in HSI, obtaining labelled samples is challenging because of the high cost associated with ground truth acquisition. Consequently, dimensionality reduction techniques, such as feature selection or feature extraction, play a vital role in addressing these challenges. Despite their importance, developing robust and effective methods for dimensionality reduction remains a significant and ongoing challenge.

In the next section, several approaches for handling all the challenges mentioned above are discussed in detail.

1.2 Background Literature

As discussed in the previous section, pixel-wise classification of HSI plays a crucial role in numerous applications. However, it faced many challenges that hinder accurate classification. In the past years, researchers have unfolded a variety of approaches to address each one of these challenges. To mitigate the drawbacks of the high dimensionality of HSI, classifiers capable of handling high dimensions are used to analyse and process the image. Dimensionality reduction techniques were also applied to HSI to improve classification performance. However, the high intra-class variability and low inter-class variability of spectral information due to environmental factors and mixed pixels continue to pose a significant challenge to classification performance. Therefore, several approaches emerge which adopted the integration of spatial and spectral information to analyse the HSI. But, finding an effective way to do this remains an ongoing research. And in the case where limited labelled samples are available, two solutions are provided in the literature. One is using a semi-supervised approach, and the other is through active learning. Semi-supervised learning exploits unlabelled samples to select certain samples for improving the reliability and the generalization in the training of a classifier. Whereas, active learning (AL) selects uncertain samples from the unlabelled pool and assigns them a label with the help of a supervisor for updating the training set of the classifier. Amidst these solutions to the different challenges mentioned above, it is important to note that the choice of the classifier used to ultimately classify the data is also a very important decision. The right classifier will fully and properly exploit the information from the preprocessed HSI data, resulting in better classification performance. The following subsection will go deeper into several literature methods that deals with the above challenges. The literature review includes dimensionality reduction, active learning and spectral-spatial classification techniques. However, the primary focus will be on sparse representation techniques and their effectiveness in classifying the HSI.

1.2.1 Dimensionality reduction

Hyperspectral remote sensing offers highly detailed image data with a wide range of spectral information, allowing the differentiation of subtle variations in ground surfaces. However, the extensive data produced by hyperspectral sensors pose challenges in analysing the data effectively. Studies have revealed that much of the high-dimensional space is empty, suggesting that the data often reside in a lower-dimensional subspace [46]. As a result, the data's dimensionality can be reduced without substantially compromising information or the ability to differentiate between various classes. Various methods in the literature aim to achieve this objective, and they can be divided into two categories, feature selection or feature extraction. These two categories are briefly discussed below.

1.2.1.1 Feature Selection

Feature selection is the task of selecting relevant attributes and removing irrelevant and redundant ones in order to obtain the best-fit subset of features without transformation[195]. For the classification problem, feature selection aims to select features that are capable of discriminating samples that belong to different classes. The selected features lead to better classification performance, lower computational cost, and better model interpretability. Feature selection can be further subdivided into three categories, filter, wrapper, and embedded.

1. Filter Method: It performs feature selection using statistical techniques that evaluate features based on their intrinsic characteristics such as variance, correlation, and other statistical measurements. The features are selected before learning the model [6, 167].

2. Wrapper Method: It uses the learning algorithm to select quality features. It iteratively selects subsets of features to test the performance of the algorithm, and the set of features that gives the best results are chosen. This process is repeated until no improvement is observed [38, 158]. This method gives better features than the filter method but at the cost of expensive

execution time.

3. Embedded Method: It has the advantage of both filter and wrapper method. Here, the feature selection process and training of the algorithm occurs parallelly. In other words, it achieves feature selection while simultaneously fitting the model [9, 256].

Under these three methods, there have been a variety of techniques dedicated to HSI. Some filter based methods used statistical measurements to rank the bands in terms of importance, as in [190], while others exploit the searching algorithm or use clustering to find the best subset of features [27, 74, 212, 262]. Under wrapper method, many classification-dependent techniques were developed which tries to optimize an objective function in order to evaluate the best bands [24, 44, 278]. And sparsity-based and deep learning based techniques are some embedded methods used to incorporate band selection into the optimization of the models [49, 89, 259]. Finally, a hybrid approach that combines the above methods is also seen in [100, 123, 258]. A detailed survey on band selection is also available in [189].

1.2.1.2 Feature Extraction

In HSI, feature extraction techniques aim to find the most important information from the data. This can be done by either highlighting key features through arithmetic operations or projecting the data onto a new feature space that enhance the discriminatory information between different classes. The new resultant feature sets often has lower dimension, making it easier to analyse. However, there are cases where it might have the same or even more dimensions than the original data. In the realm of HSI, both supervised and unsupervised feature extraction techniques are present. Some supervised techniques include discriminant analysis feature extraction (DAFE) [175], non-parametric weighted feature extraction (NWFE) [115], cosine-based non-parametric feature extraction (CNFE) [250], feature space discriminative analysis (FSDA) [77] and rough-set-based [208]. On the other hand, unsupervised approaches include techniques such as principal component analysis (PCA) [242] and independent component analysis (ICA) [35] with their kernelized versions, minimum noise fraction (MNF) [156], isometric mapping (ISOMAP) [213] and sparse and smooth low-rank analysis (SSLRA) [180]. Among these techniques, PCA is found to be the most popular choice due to its simplicity, robustness, and fast computation. Similarly, in this thesis, PCA was used to reduce the dimensions of HSI, and more about it will be described below.

PCA is an unsupervised method to reduce the dimensionality of HSI data. Its primary objective is to identify the principal components of the HSI, in which the first component retains the maximum amount of information and the subsequent components contain the remaining information in decreasing order. Afterwards, the original data undergo projection onto a new feature space with lower dimensions using a selected subset of these principal components.

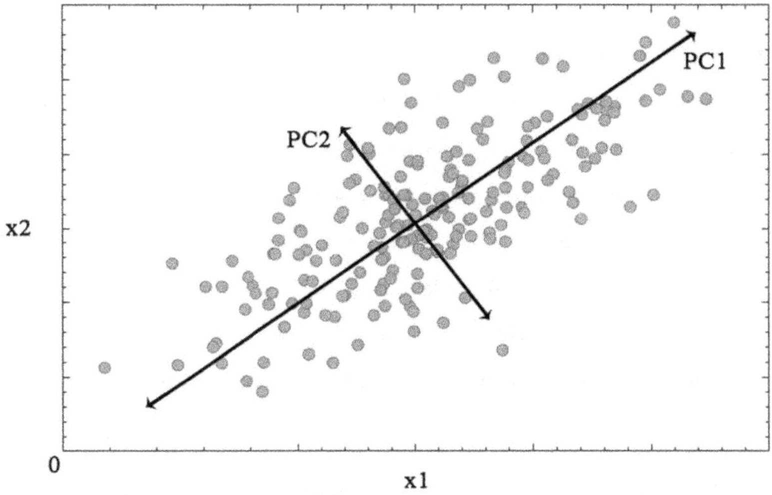

Figure 1-3: Principal Component Analysis

In greater detail, we have HSI $\mathbf{H}$ of size $P \times Q \times B$, where $P \times Q$ are the spatial dimensions and B is the spectral dimension. To calculate the principal components (PCs), the image is reshaped into a matrix χ of size $T \times B$, where,

$T = P \times Q$ gives the total number of pixels in the image. The new features are then extracted from χ using the following steps.

- Firstly, the range of variables is calculated and standardized to analyse the contribution of each variable equally. If μ_i is the mean of each feature f_i, $i = 1, 2, \ldots, B$, and β_i is its standard deviation, the standardized dataset χ_{new} is given as:

$$\chi_{new} = \frac{f_i - \mu_i}{\beta_i} \tag{1.1}$$

- Secondly, the covariance matrix between each pair of features in χ_{new} are calculated to obtain their intercorrelation information. The covariance matrix $COV(i, j)$ is calculated as:

$$COV(i, j) = \frac{\sum f_i * f_j}{T} \quad where, i, j = 1, 2, \ldots, B \tag{1.2}$$

- Thirdly, the eigenvectors E_{vec}, and eigenvalues E_{val} are computed from $COV(i, j)$ in order to determine the principal components of the data. E_{vec} represents the principal components (PCs) and they illustrate the direction of the axes where there is the most variance. And E_{val} holds the coefficients of each eigenvector in E_{vec}, which gives the amount of variance carried in each PC. The eigenvectors are ranked in descending order of eigenvalues. This means that the first vector holds the maximum variance or information, the second holds the maximum remaining information, and so on.

- Next, for dimensionality reduction, a new PC matrix is created by choosing only the first l ($l < B$) principal components that hold the maximum information. This new matrix E^l_{vec} of size $B \times l$ holds the new axes where the original data will be projected.

- Finally, in the last step, the original data χ_{new} is projected onto the new axes of the principal components to form χ'_{new}. This is then reshaped back to the original spatial dimension to obtain $\mathbf{I} \in \mathbb{R}^{P \times Q \times l}$.

$$\chi'_{new} = \chi_{new} * \mathrm{E}^{l}_{vec} \tag{1.3}$$

In this way, PCA transformed the high dimensionality **H** to low dimensionality **I** with l dimensional features. Figure 1-3 illustrates the two principal axes across the maximum and the second maximum variance of the simulated data.

1.2.2 Incorporation of spatial information for analysis of HSI

Dimensionality reduction methods have been instrumental in addressing the challenge of dealing with the high-dimensionality of HSI. However, HSI remains noisy due to low spatial resolution and various environmental factors. This noise contributes to high intraclass variability and low interclass variability, resulting in poor discrimination of pixels and, subsequently, poor classification accuracy in images. To counteract these limitations, spatial information is integrated into the analysis of HSI. The underlying concept is that when spectral features alone prove insufficient to distinguish between pixels of different classes, particularly those with similar spectral signatures, incorporating information from neighbouring pixels can aid in discrimination. There are several ways in which spatial information can be used to classify the HSI [83, 97]. These are divided into three categories: preprocessing based approaches, integration based approaches and post-processing based approaches.

Preprocessing based approaches

Preprocessing based approaches in HSI analysis begin by extracting spatial information before classification. These methods generally follow a two-step process: first, the spectral-spatial features are extracted to represent the pixels within the HSI. Second, these features are then classified using any traditional classifier such as SVM, sparse representation classification (SRC), random forest etc. In the literature, several popular methods follow this approach, such as object-based methods[60, 266], filter-based methods [66, 173, 176], mathematical morphology based [41, 229]etc. To fully understand how this approach works, let's examine how the mathematical morphology (MM) framework operate in gathering spatial information from HSI.

The fundamental operators in MM are dilation $\delta_e(\mathrm{I})$ and erosion, $\varepsilon_e(\mathrm{I})$ which are applied on an image I to filter bright/dark objects. These operators rely on a small fixed shape structuring element, e. By combining these operators, other morphological operators such as opening ($\gamma_e(\mathrm{I})$), closing ($\phi_e(\mathrm{I})$), opening by reconstruction ($\gamma_R(\mathrm{I})$) and closing by reconstruction ($\phi_R(\mathrm{I})$) are formed [230]. Among these, the reconstruction approach has demonstrated better preservation of object shapes and is hence often preferred. Since these operators rely on the size of one structuring element, therefore the filter image produce may remove some important objects from the original image leading to loss of information. Hence, to overcome this, multiscale structuring elements are considered to produce a collection of filter images that captures objects of various sizes present in the image. The filter images obtained by using $\gamma_R(\mathrm{I})$ are called opening profile or granulometry, and those obtained by using $\phi_R(\mathrm{I})$ are called closing profile or anti-granulometry. The combination of these two sets of filter images along with the original image form a Morphological Profile (MP). This can be represented as follows.

$$MP(\mathrm{I}) = \{\gamma_R^{\lambda_i}(\mathrm{I}), \mathrm{I}, \phi_R^{\lambda_i}(\mathrm{I})\} \tag{1.4}$$

where λ_i are the sizes of multiscale structuring elements.

Extended Morphological Profile (EMP)

For a HSI **H**, MP was generated using the first principal component (PC). Although the first PC carries the maximum variation, important information may be present in other PCs as well. Therefore, in [171], an extended morphological profile (EMP) was built from multiple PCs as follows.

$$EMP(\mathbf{H}) = \{MP(\mathrm{PC}_1), MP(\mathrm{PC}_2), \ldots, MP(\mathrm{PC}_l)\} \quad (1.5)$$

where, l is the number of principal component. This combination of size variations, shape information and spectral data are more detailed and offers rich and better spatial information than traditional MPs. This profile is then used by the classifier to enhanced the classification accuracy [61]. In the literature, several variants and modification were made to enhance it even further. In [129] and [210] different dimension reduction techniques were used instead of PCA to extract the EMP from HSI. This potentially captures a wider range of valuable information from the image. The original EMP was created using a single shape structuring elements, and hence it may fail to capture objects of different shapes present in the image. Therefore, in addition to various sizes, structuring elements of various shapes were utilized in [144] to address the issue. Furthermore, wavelets were also used in [142, 177] to improve the quality of spatial information. The results obtained show a good improvement in classification performance.

As observed from its use in the literature, EMP has proven effective in capturing the variation of structures in different scales within the image. But due to its dependency in the structuring elements, it cannot model objects based on other geometrical and textural features. To overcome this limitation, morphological attribute filters (AFs) were proposed instead of the traditional operators to create a better spatial profile called Extended Morphological Attribute Profile (EMAP).

Extended Morphological Attribute Profile (EMAP)

Attribute filters (AFs) are a set of connected operators designed for the analysis of an image's connected components [18]. Their purpose is to selectively remove connected components that do not meet a specified threshold based on an attribute. The generation of a filtered image using AFs comprises three key steps [187]. Initially, a tree structure is constructed to represent the connected components of the input (grayscale) image. Subsequently, a filtering operation is performed by merging specific nodes within this tree that do not meet the criterion with their respective parent nodes. Finally, the processed tree is reconstructed to produce the filtered output image. In the literature, the max-tree and min-tree representations are commonly used to model the connected components of the input image. These three steps are explained in detail below.

Max-tree creation: This phase describes how a max-tree is created with just two steps, repeated recursively. The first step is called the *binarization* step, and it splits the image into 'local background set' (pixels with the lowest intensity) and 'local background complement set' (all other pixels). And the second step is called the *connected component definition*, which identifies the connected components in the local background complement set in order to form the child nodes. This procedure is applied recursively to each of these child nodes, resulting in the construction of a tree wherein each node corresponds to a distinct connected component within the image. Figure 1-4 shows a toy image that explains in detail the construction of max-tree and the generation of filtered image using *area* attribute.

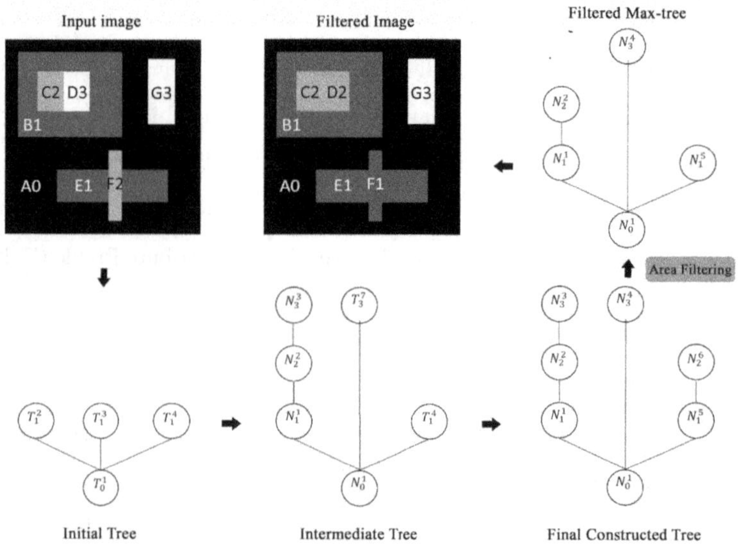

Figure 1-4: Construction of max-tree and filter image obtained from it.

The image contains many connected components labelled with alphabets

$\{A, B, C, D, E, F, G\}$ and numbers $\{0, 1, 2, 3\}$ that represent their gray value. To filter the image, the *area* attribute with $\lambda = 25$ as the threshold is considered, and for this example, we assume that the areas of the connected components D3 and F2 are below 25 pixels. Initially, the minimum gray value 0 is considered as the threshold value ($v_g = 0$) for *binarization* step. This created the local background set {A0} with pixel intensity 0 and the local background complement set {B1, C2, D3, E1, F2, G3} containing all other pixels. Applying the *connected component definition* to the local background complement set, three child nodes were generated: $T_1^1 = \{B1, C2, D3\}$, $T_1^2 = \{E1, F2\}$ and $T_1^3 = \{G3\}$. Next, taking T_1^1 as input image and applying the same two-fold procedure with the threshold $v_g = 1$, the *binarization* step generates the local background set {B1} and the local background complement set { C2, D3}. The node T_1^1 is then converted to the permanent node N_1^1. The two-step process is then repeated for each child node, until all connected components are analysed and the final max-tree is built.

Filtering of Max-Tree: The filtering process analyses each node N_i^j by assessing the value of a particular attribute (*area*). For each node, the *area* attribute is compared to the threshold $\lambda = 25$. The node is merged to the parent if the value is less than λ, else it is retained. From the figure, it can be seen that the node N_3^3 and N_2^6 is merged to the parent node since their *area* attribute is lesser than the threshold, while the rest were kept as they were.

Image Restitution: The last step of the filtering process consists of transforming the output max-tree into a filter image. This is done by assigning each pixel the gray-level value of the node it belongs to. From the figure, it can be observed that the background pixels belonging to node N_1^5 is assigned the gray-value 1 and the pixels belonging to node N_2^2 is assigned the gray-value 2. This entire process is repeated for each pixel in the image to produce the filtered image.

Now, in order to create the profile from HSI, max-tree and min-tree with g different thresholds (i.e., $\lambda_1 < \lambda_2, \ldots, < \lambda_g$) are constructed to generate $2g$ filtered images. The filtered images obtained using max-tree are called thinning profile since they filter bright objects, and vice versa the filtered images obtained using min-tree are called thickening profile. Both these profile combine with the original principal components formed the Extended Attribute Profile (EAP) [40, 42]. It is represented as follows:

$$EAP(\mathbf{H}) = \{AP(PC_1), AP(PC_2), \dots AP(PC_l)\} \tag{1.6a}$$

$$where, AP(PC_i) = \{\gamma_{\lambda_1}(PC_i), \dots, \gamma_{\lambda_S}(PC_i), PC_i, \phi_{\lambda_1}(PC_i), \dots, \phi_{\lambda_g}(PC_i)\} \tag{1.6b}$$

While Extended Attribute Profiles (EAPs) capture spatial information through a single attribute (like *area*), this limits the amount of information that can be extracted. To address this, the researchers developed EMAPs [39]. EMAPs are build on EAPs by considering several attributes simultaneously such as *area*, *standard deviation*, etc. By incorporating multiple attributes, EMAPs capture a richer and more comprehensive picture of the spatial information within the image [96, 200]. An EMAP for the HSI **H** can be defined as below.

$$EMAP(\mathbf{H}) = \{EAP_{a_1}(\mathbf{H}), EAP_{a_2}(\mathbf{H}), \dots, EAP_{a_{N_a}}(\mathbf{H})\} \tag{1.7}$$

Here, a_i are the different attributes and N_a is the number of attributes.

Integration based approaches

In integrated-based methodologies for HSI classification, the classifier directly incorporate the contextual information associated with individual pixels to perform the classification task. This involves the exploitation of both spectral and spatial features during the classification process. The main assumption in these approaches is that the pixels within the same spatial neighbourhood belong to the same class. There are various ways to capture this contextual information. The three most common ways are: fixed-size window, adaptive window and hybrid.

Fixed-size square window: It is the most common approach used to extract contextual information from a pixel. These windows typically have symmetrical dimensions, commonly seen in odd sizes such as $3 \times 3, 5 \times 5, 7 \times 7, \ldots$ and so on. In [21, 118], these windows serve the purpose of identifying both the first and second-order neighbourhood systems. And in[29], a fixed-size window was implemented to seamlessly integrate spatial information into the sparse representation classifier (SRC) to optimize its performance. Since then, many variants of this technique have been subsequently developed to refine the classification process [222, 253]. Additionally, many deep learning models also adopted this approach to facilitate classification [159, 260].

Adaptive window: Although the fixed-sized square window is simple and effective in gathering spatial information, in many cases, however, it does not indicate a correct spatial neighbourhood of a pixel. As a result, several superpixel segmentation-based models were developed to overcome this [121, 221]. All these models first apply a segmentation technique to group together the neighbour pixels that have similar characteristics using one or more principal components. The discriminative power of the obtained spatial information relies on how well the neighbouring pixels are grouped together. One method used for this purpose is Simple Linear Iterative Clustering (SLIC).

SLIC decomposes HSI into homogeneous segments in the CIELAB color space using their first three principal components (PCs). [185, 206]. It generate super-pixels by clustering pixel based on color similarity and proximity. The algorithm starts by creating n seed points. In the second step, the algorithm scans the area around each seed point to find a group of pixels that are close to the seed and classifies them as belonging to the seed's category. Finally, in the third step, the average values of all pixels within each superpixel were computed to establish the next n cluster centers. Steps two and three are then repeated until convergence.

In SLIC, a pixel y is represented using five dimensions, $[l, a, b, g^x, g^z]$, (l, a, b) are its coordinates in the HSV space and (g^x, g^z) are its spatial coordinates. If d_{lab} be the distance for measuring colour similarity and $d_{g^x g^z}$ be the distance for measuring proximity between j^{th} seed and pixel y_i, then their total distance D_{slic}

is shown below.

$$d_{lab} = \sqrt{(l_j - l_i)^2 + (a_j - a_i)^2 + (b_j - b_i)^2}$$

$$d_{g^x g^z} = \sqrt{(g_j^x - g_i^x)^2 + (g_j^x - g_i^y)^2}$$

$$D_{slic} = d_{lab} + \frac{\tau}{\theta} d_{g^x g^z}$$

where τ adjust the weight of $d_{g^x g^z}$ and θ represents the side length of each superpixel calculated as $\theta = \sqrt{T/n}$, where T denotes the total number of pixels in the image.

Hybrid: The use of a fixed-size window is a simplistic approach for capturing spatial contextual information. Whereas in superpixel based methods, the determination of the optimum number of segments present in the image is a non-trivial problem, since the shape and size of the superpixels generated by the segmentation techniques strongly depend on the number of segments. Therefore, like the fixed-size based models, the superpixel based models require prior information for defining the appropriate shapes of the windows. To mitigate this drawback, several variants of the above methods were developed that combined multiple scales of such windows to gather contextual information such as Multiscale Adaptive Sparse Representation Classification (MASRC) [56], Multiscale Superpixel Sparse Representation Classification (MSSRC) [268], and Adaptive MultiScale Segmentations (AMS) [117]. And other variants, such as Superpixel-to-Pixel Weighting Distance (SWPD) [223], Robust Dual-Stage Spatial Embedding (RDSSE) [192], used more complex ideas to model spatial information.

Post-processing based approaches

Post-processing based approaches are simply those methods that aim to enhance the classification accuracy by refining the labels in a classified image using spatial information. These approaches typically have two steps. First, a pixel-wise classification of the HSI is performed and then the spatial dependency of the pixels are utilized in the next step to improve the accuracy. In the literature, several methods have been developed to establish image boundaries and capture this spatial dependency. These methods can be classified into categories such as segmentation based, filter based, relaxation based and random field approaches [91]. Various techniques exist in the literature to establish image boundaries and capture this spatial dependency, including segmentation-based, filter-based, relaxation-based, and random field approaches.. In segmentation based approaches, the segmentation map is used to smoothen the classification map. Specifically, the dominant class label within a segment are assigned to all pixels within it [105, 211, 276]. Filter based approaches consider the probabilistic output of the classifier and, with the help of a moving window, they filter this output to get the final classification map [53, 76, 136]. Relaxation based approaches use continuous and probabilistic relaxation techniques to reduce noise and improve classification accuracy by correcting both spectral and spatial distortions. [64, 65, 198].Finally, random field approaches utilize Markov Random Field (MRF) to model spatial relationships between pixels and refine the classification map through smoothing. [25, 102, 157]. One example of these approaches can be seen in [106], where a support vector machine (SVM) classifier is initially applied to the HSI to generate multiple probability maps. Subsequently, edge-preserving filtering (EPF) is performed on each of these probability maps to refine them. The final class assignment for each pixel is then determined based on the maximum probability value across the filtered maps.

Deep Learning Approaches

Recently, deep learning has become a growing trend in HSI analysis due to its strong performance. Unlike traditional hand-crafted techniques, deep learning automatically extracts meaningful features from raw data through multiple hierarchical layers. Early layers capture basic features like edges and textures, while deeper layers identify more complex patterns. This automatic learning process makes deep learning well-suited to handle diverse scenarios[73, 125, 179].

Over the past decade, many deep learning models have been developed for HSI classification. One of the earliest models was introduced by Chen et al., and it utilized stacked autoencoders (SAE) to derive high-level features from HSI data for classification [31]. Seeing this success, several other works were published in the literature based on stack auto encoder (SAE) for HSI classification [5, 126, 277].

Another popular deep learning approach is Convolution Neural Networks. They became widely used in land use and land cover (LULC) classification due to their effective handling of HSIs [68, 104, 239]. CNNs apply multiple convolutional operations across different spectral wavelengths to create numerous feature maps. These maps capture better spatial relationships among neighboring pixels, leading to enhanced spatial-spectral feature representation than those obtained from SAEs and improved classification accuracy. However, CNN due their intricate architecture demand substantial parameter tuning and computational resources, which potentially diminish their suitability for deployment in resource-limited environments. Furthermore, CNN failed to capture global relationships since they rely on kernels to capture spatial relationship.

Therefore, to address these issues several other deep learning architectures were developed. Lightweight CNN such as in [2] were developed which requires fewer parameters that significantly reduce the convergence time while providing better accuracy. In [178, 183, 199], Squeeze-and-Excitation Networks (SENet) and related channel-attention mechanisms were introduced to strengthen feature expressiveness within CNN-based models. SENets adaptively recalibrate channel-wise feature responses by emphasizing informative spectral bands and suppressing redundant ones. This enhances the discriminative power of spectral–spatial features while adding only minimal computational cost, making them suitable for improving CNN performance without significantly increasing model complexity. Furthermore, to deal with the failure to capture global relationships, Graph Convolution Network (GCN) were developed which unlike CNN that works on pixelgrid structures and local receptive fields, GCN works on graph structures. This enables the model to capture long-range dependencies and global contextual information that cannot be learned through standard convolutions [50, 88, 101]. To further improve global modelling, several authors uses transformers architectures [85, 184, 205]. These models use self-attention mechanisms that allow every pixel (or patch) to interact with every other pixel, enabling the network to learn global spectral and spatial dependencies efficiently. This makes Transformers highly effective for complex HSI scenes with irregular patterns or large intra-class variability.

1.2.3 Active learning for hyperspectral image classification

HSIs are effective in many applications such as environmental monitoring, crops analysis, land cover analysis, and many more. This has resulted in the development of many supervised methods. As seen above, several methods have been proposed to curb the "*curse of dimensionality*" and enhance relevant discriminative information. However, supervised methods still require quality and adequate labelled samples for training to build a good classifier. This turns out to be expensive and time-consuming, as proper labelling requires either field survey or photo interpretation by the experts. Therefore, to address these problems, active learning methods were developed.

Active learning (AL) is an approach in which the learning algorithm engages with an expert to label data according to desired class through interactive querying. The objective is to strategically identify and incorporate a limited number of informative samples into the labelled (training) set, with an aim to decrease labelling expenses while improving the classification performance [163]. Figure 1-5 illustrates a detailed framework of AL.

At the beginning, a few randomly chosen labelled samples are added to the labelled pool. With the help of this set, the AL algorithm iteratively applies the query function to the unlabelled pool to obtain the h most informative data samples. These samples are then passed to the supervisor for labelling. After labelling

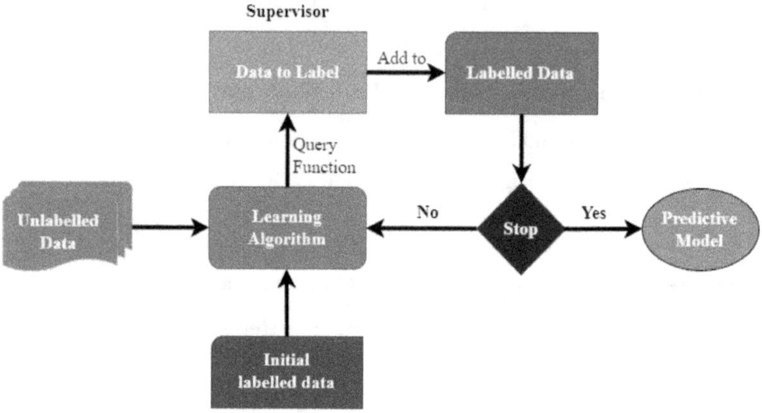

Figure 1-5: Illustration of the active learning (AL) framework.

them with the correct class, they are then added to the labelled pool. This process is repeated until the stopping condition is met, and then the final labelled samples obtained are used by the predictive model for performance analysis. Algorithm 1 shows a basic pseudocode for active learning (AL).

Algorithm 1 Active Learning

Input: labelled Pool L^P; Unlabelled Pool U^P; Query Function F_Q ; h parameter;

Add few randomly chosen labelled samples to L^P
repeat:
    Train the model using labelled samples from L^P.
    For each data sample $i \in U^P$, compute informative measure using F_Q.
    Select the h informative data samples from U^P.
    Assign them the appropriate class label with the help of supervisor.
    Add them to L^P
until stopping criterion is met.

AL approaches can be categorized in two ways. One is on the basis of how many samples are selected per iteration, and the other is on how the uncertainty of the unlabelled samples is defined. In the first way, AL methods are categorized into single mode and batch mode [155]. Single mode AL selects the single informative sample, whereas batch mode AL selects multiple informative samples at each iteration for labelling. Since retraining the model for every single sample is slow, remote sensing applications tend to prefer batch mode. The second way is a more popular approach among researchers. It is known that the most fundamental part of active learning (AL) is designing a query function that identifies the most informative samples for labeling. This function use various criteria to make their choices. In the literature, AL methods are typically classified into three categories based on the criteria they adopt. These possible criteria are uncertainty, diversity, and hybrid. The uncertainty criterion measures the confidence of a sample in belonging to a particular class. The diversity criterion measures the dissimilarity of uncertain samples from the labelled samples. The hybrid criteria include a combination of both uncertainty and diversity criteria along with other criterion as well, such as cluster assumption, spatial information, etc [165, 214].

Uncertainty Criterion

The uncertainty criterion is a function that identifies unlabelled samples located near the boundaries of certain classes. There are many ways to compute the uncertainty, as shown in the literature and they can be divided into four more subcategories: posterior probability-based, margin-based, committee-based, and learning-based [161, 226].

Posterior probabilities based AL are those that utilize supervised models trained on labelled datasets to estimate the probability of class predictions for unlabelled data. The predicted posterior probability of unlabelled samples are used to represent the prediction's uncertainty. One commonly used technique is known as breaking ties (BT) [143]. It selects the uncertain samples based on the difference in the predicted probabilities of the two classes. In binary classification, the sample is considered the most uncertain if its probabilities are close to 0.5 for both classes. In a multi-class situation, the sample deemed uncertain is the one showing the smallest difference between the highest predicted probabilities of the two classes. It is calculated as follows:

$$y^{BT} = \arg\min_{y_i \in \mathrm{U^P}} \left[\max_{c \in C} p(\hat{c} = c|y_i) - \max_{c \in C \backslash c^+} p(\hat{c} = c|y_i) \right] \tag{1.8}$$

where, $p(\hat{c} = c|y_i)$ is the predicted posterior probabilities of a sample y_i as belonging to a class c and the most probable class for y_i is denoted by c^+.

The margin based AL are those that used SVM as the underlying learning model [47, 164, 234]. SVM uses hyperplanes as decision boundaries to separate samples between different classes. This makes them well-suited for active learning because unlabelled samples whose distances are closer to the hyperplane have low classification confidence and hence are considered uncertain by the model. This distance of an unlabelled sample to the hyperplane is computed as:

$$f(y_i) = \sum_{j=1}^{N_s} \alpha_j c_j K(y_i, y_j) + b \tag{1.9}$$

where, N_s is the number of support vectors, c_j is the class of support vector y_j and $K(y_i, y_j)$ is the kernel function that calculate the similarity between y_i and support vector y_j.

A popular technique that use this strategy is called margin sampling (MS) [149, 225]. It selects unlabelled samples that are likely to become support vectors for labelling. These are the samples according to this strategy that have the lowest classification confidence (CC) and hence are considered uncertain. Certain modifications were also made to this in [34, 279], to avoid selecting samples that will not become support vectors. In a multi-class one against all (OAA) scenario, the distance from each unlabelled sample to each hyperplane of C different classes are computed, and the minimum distance recorded is considered as its classification confidence (CC). The sample with the minimum CC is considered uncertain.

$$y^{MS} = \arg\min_{y_i \in \mathrm{U}^{\mathrm{P}}} \left[\min_{j=1,2,\ldots,C} f_j(y_i) \right] \tag{1.10}$$

The next subcategory of uncertainty criterion is called committee based AL [84, 108, 191]. These methods make a committee and quantifies the uncertainty of unlabelled sample based on multiple supervised learning models. Here, each learning algorithm in the committee takes different hypothesis about the classification problem, and they predict each unlabelled sample independently. Then the sample whose labels assignment have the maximum disagreement are considered uncertain. In [225], an Entropy Query by Bagging (EQB) was proposed to build the committee using SVM classifier. In this technique, initially, Q training sets are built by randomly selecting from the labelled set. Each set is then used to train the classifier to predict the unlabelled samples. At the end of the procedure, each unlabelled sample receives Q labellings. Finally, the entropy H_{BAG} of the prediction distribution is utilized to identify the sample with the highest disagreement. This entropy H_{BAG} of unlabelled pixel y_i is computed as

$$H_{BAG}(y_i) = -\sum_{k=1}^{N_{y_i}} p^{BAG}(\hat{c} = c_k|y_i) log\left[p^{BAG}(\hat{c} = c_k|y_i)\right] \tag{1.11a}$$

$$where \quad p^{BAG}(\hat{c} = c_k|y_i) = \frac{\sum_{q=1}^{Q} \delta(\hat{c}_{i,q}, c_k)}{\sum_{q=1}^{Q} \sum_{j=1}^{N_{y_i}} \delta(\hat{c}_{i,q}, c_j)} \tag{1.11b}$$

Here, in Eqn.1.11a and Eqn.1.11b N_{y_i} represents the number of distinct classes predicted for the sample y_i constrained by $1 \geq N_{y_i} \geq C$, the $\delta(\hat{c}_{i,w}, c_j)$ operator returns 1 if the qth classifier assigns the class label c_j to the sample y_i, and 0 otherwise. Finally, $p^{BAG}(\hat{c} = C_k|y_i)$ denotes the probability that the committee of Q classifiers predicts c_k as the class label for y_i.

In [36], this measure has been further normalized to constrain it based on the number of classes predicted by the committee. By using the normalized entropy query-by-bagging (nEQB) approach, the most uncertain sample can be identified as follows.

$$y^{nEQB} = \underset{y_i \in \mathrm{U^P}}{\arg\max} \left\{ \frac{H_{BAG}(y_i)}{log(N_{y_i})} \right\} \tag{1.12}$$

Recently, learning-based AL has been introduced as a solution to address the limitations of heuristic-based AL approaches [87, 110]. The performance of the various heuristics based AL methods is limited by its dependency on the dataset complexity and the learning model. Therefore, to overcome this, the learning-based AL methods were proposed with the reinforcement learning (RL) framework. An example of this is an Active Learning By Learning (ALBL) method developed in [87]. It solves the task of AL by using a multi armed bandit technique called EXP4.P. Given a budget (e.g. number of iterations) and Q learning algorithms, the objective of the technique is to sequentially decide which learning algorithm to use that will determine the uncertain sample while also maximizing the total rewards earned.

EXP4.P adaptively maintains a weight vector $w(t)$ in iteration t, where the qth component $w_q(t)$ is the non-negative weight of the qth learning algorithm. The weight vector $w(t)$ is then scaled to a probability vector $p(t) \in [p_{min} 1]$ with some parameter $p_{min} > 0$. EXP4.P then use $p(t)$ to choose the learning algorithm. Next, the chosen algorithm then makes a probabilistic query using a query vector $\psi^k(t) \in [0, 1]^{N_u}$, where N_u is the number of unlabelled samples and its ith component $\psi_i^q(t)$ indicates the preference of the qth algorithm on querying the label of $y_i \in \mathrm{U^P}$. For simplicity, the two probabilistic steps can be combined in order to directly sample the uncertain sample. The function can be formulated as follows.

$$y_{ALBL} = \underset{y_i \in \mathrm{U^P}}{\arg\max} \left\{ \sum_{q=1}^{Q} p^q(t) \psi_i^q(t) \right\} \tag{1.13}$$

Diversity Criterion

In AL, diversity criterion are those functions that allow the model to choose non-redundant uncertain samples[225, 241, 255]. Redundant samples don't significantly enhance the discriminative and representative power of the labelled set. Therefore, to solve this problem, this approach rank the samples to identify diverse samples using a diversity criterion. Several methods have been developed for this, such as clustering based approaches like K-means, Kernel K-means and Self Organizing Map (SOM) [47, 164] and region based approaches like Angular Based Diversity (ABD) and Region Partitioning (RP) [20, 94].

ABD aims to identify diverse samples based on the angular distances between the samples. This distance between each pair of samples (y_i, y_j) is measured using the cosine distances in kernel space, as follows.

$$ABD(y_i, y_j) = \frac{K(y_i, y_j)}{\sqrt{K(y_i, y_i)K(y_j, y_j)}} \tag{1.14}$$

A higher value of $ABD(y_i, y_j)$ indicates that the distance is large, and hence they are non-redundant. So samples that have high values are considered as informative samples.

Region partitioning (RP) is an SVM based diversity criterion. Using the hyperplanes of the learned SVM, it divides the space of uncertain samples into different regions (zones). Samples that are in the same region are considered redundant, while those in different regions are non-redundant. Depending on the number of samples per batch, this approach selects first those samples whose regions they belong to are furthest from each other and then subsequently select samples from adjacent regions.

Hybrid Criteria

Hybrid criteria aim to combine the above two criteria together in order to get better informative samples that improve the classification performance. There are several methods in the literature that use this approach, such as multi class level uncertainty with kernel k-means (MCLU-KK), multi class level uncertainty with angular based diversity (MCLU-ABD), margin sampling with region partition (MS-RP) etc. First, m samples are selected using *criterion 1* (e.g. uncertainty criterion) then a *criterion 2* (e.g. diversity criterion) is applied to these h samples to identify $m(m < h)$ informative samples.

In addition to this, researchers have also explored other criteria that are specific to remote sensing images [127, 153]. One approach is superpixel, through which the relative position of each unlabelled pixel in the image is located, and this is used when selecting informative samples. Basically, informative samples belonging to different superpixels are selected, since those lying within the same superpixels are considered redundant. Another method is the cluster assumption, which assumes that the decision boundary usually lies in the low density region, and hence the sample selected from such a region will be more informative [162]. And finally, the edge gradient, which incorporates edge information into the query function [188]. It is based on the principle that samples lying on the edges are most difficult to classify, and hence they are considered informative.

1.2.4 Sparse Representation Classification for the analysis of HSI

As seen in the literature presented above, various methods have been proposed to tackle the challenges associated with HSI classification. One key element in the classification process is the classifier itself. The choice of classifier is very crucial, as it directly influences the success of the experiment, measured by accuracy, precision, computational efficiency, and other relevant metrics. Among the various traditional classifiers that exist, the SRC have demonstrated their robustness in various applications. As mentioned earlier, it offers many advantages over other classifiers, such as its inherent lazy learning nature, minimal computational requirements, improved interpretability, and seamless integration of spatial information. These advantageous characteristics show that SRC has great potential and hence has been selected as a based model for classifying the HSI in this thesis. More details about the model are presented below.

Sparse Representation Classification (SRC)

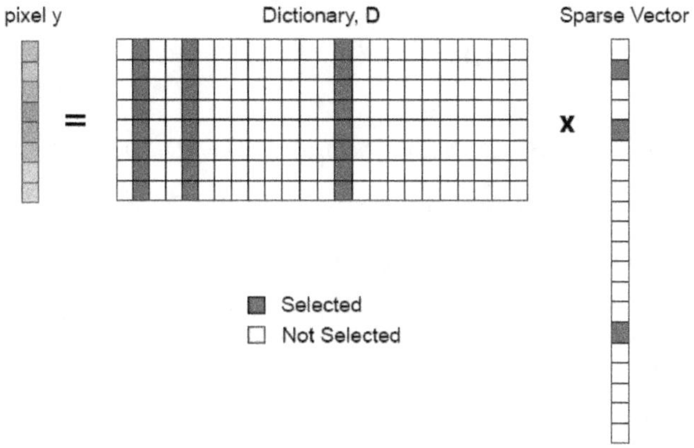

Figure 1-6: Sparse Representation Classification (SRC)

SRC is a specific application of sparse coding and was introduced in [243] for face recognition. It provided a very strong performance on various face recognition datasets and has been widely used since then for various applications, including HSI classification [169, 246, 273]. It is based on the idea that every unlabelled pixel can be approximately represented by similar labelled pixels, which are called the basis or atoms in a dictionary. Specifically, SRC initially represents an unlabelled pixel as a linear combination of a few labelled pixels (training samples) in a dictionary that belongs to different classes. This is done by finding labelled samples that are strongly correlated to the unlabelled pixel. The selected labelled pixels and their weights (sparse coefficients) approximate the unlabelled pixel. Finally, the residue between the unlabelled pixels and approximate pixels obtained from the labelled samples of each class is calculated to assign the class label [264].

For an HSI **H**, the strategy of SRC involves finding a linear combination of atoms for an unknown pixel $y \in \mathbb{R}^B$ such that:

$$y = \mathrm{D}_1\alpha_1 + \mathrm{D}_2\alpha_2 + \cdots + \mathrm{D}_\mathrm{C}\alpha_\mathrm{C}$$

$$y = [\mathrm{D}_1\mathrm{D}_2 \ldots \mathrm{D}_\mathrm{C}] \begin{bmatrix} \alpha_1 \\ \alpha_2 \\ \vdots \\ \alpha_C \end{bmatrix}$$

$$y = \mathrm{D}\alpha \tag{1.15}$$

The dictionary D is a $B \times N$ matrix defined as $\mathrm{D} = [\mathrm{D}_1, \mathrm{D}_2, ..., \mathrm{D}_C]$, where, D_i represents the atoms taken from the ith class and C is the total number of classes. The sparse vector α contains the sparse coefficients (represented by non-zero entries) of a particular atom. This vector can be determined by solving the following optimization problem:

$$\hat{\alpha} = \arg\min_{\alpha} \|y - \mathrm{D}\alpha\|_2 \quad s.t \quad \|\alpha\|_0 < K \tag{1.16}$$

where, K, $\|\alpha\|_0$ and $\|.\|_2$ represent the level of sparsity, number of sparse coefficients and l_2-norm respectively. The above optimization problem can be solved using the greedy algorithm or basis pursuit. Upon obtaining the estimated sparse vector $\hat{\alpha}$, the class label $\hat{c}$ of the unlabelled pixel y is determined using the following equation:

$$\hat{c} = \arg\min_{i=1,2,\ldots,C} \|y - \mathrm{D_i}\hat{\alpha_\mathrm{i}}\|_2 \tag{1.17}$$

From equations 1.15 and 1.16, it can be seen that the performance of SRC rely heavily on two factors: the quality of the labelled pixels (atoms) in the dictionary D and quality of unlabelled pixels to be classified. However, HSI pixels are often noisy, and they have high correlation with other classes, hence the unlabelled pixels may give false representation of the actual class and the atoms used in the dictionary may not accurately represent their own class. In the literature, researchers have tackled this challenge with two solutions. One involves integrating spatial information using Joint Sparse Representation Classification (JSRC). The other is dictionary learning through K Singular Value Decomposition (K-SVD), whose aim is to learn a more compact, informative and representative dictionary.

Joint Sparse Representation Classification (JSRC)

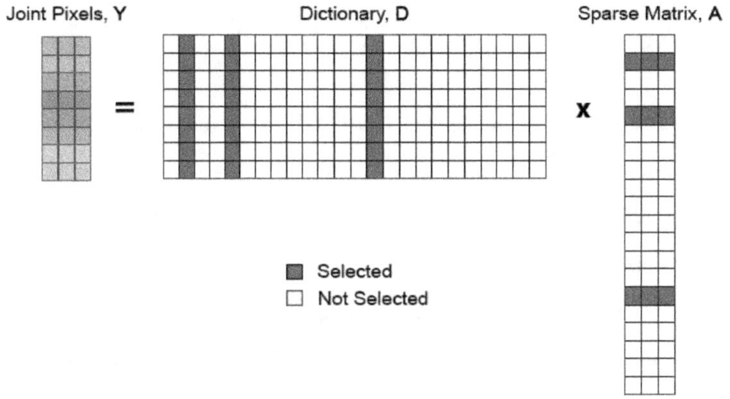

Figure 1-7: Joint Sparse Representation Classification (SRC)

The Joint Sparse Representation Classification (JSRC) model, a generalization of SRC, incorporates spectral and spatial contextual information for improved classification [29]. It assumes that neighboring pixels of an unknown pixel can be represented by the same dictionary atoms, implying that their sparse vectors share the same sparsity pattern. In other words, the sparse vectors of the neighbouring pixels may have different coefficients, but they share the same sparsity pattern. If $\mathrm{Y} \in \mathbb{R}^{B \times R}$ be a matrix containing unknown pixel y and its neighbouring pixels, then according to JSRC, Y can be represented as:

$$\mathrm{Y} = \mathrm{DA} \tag{1.18}$$

where, A contains the sparse vectors α of each pixel in the neighbourhood. Now, using the dictionary D, the sparse representation A can be obtained by solving the following optimization problem:

$$\hat{\mathrm{A}} = \arg\min_{\mathrm{A}} \|\mathrm{Y} - \mathrm{DA}\|_{\mathrm{F}} \quad \textit{subject to} \ \|\mathrm{A}\|_{row,0} < K \tag{1.19}$$

Here, $\|\mathrm{A}\|_{row,0}$ represents the number of non-zero rows of A. After the sparse representation is recovered, the class label $\hat{c}$ for the unlabelled sample y is computed as follows:

$$\hat{c} = \arg\min_{i} \|\mathrm{Y} - \mathrm{D}_i\hat{\mathrm{A}}_i\|_F \quad i \in 1, 2, 3, .., C \tag{1.20}$$

where $\hat{\mathrm{A}}_i$ represents the sparse coefficient of D_i. The JSRC model has resulted in more accurate sparse coefficients and reduce the impact of noisy pixels on the final results. This effectiveness has led to its widespread adoption in recent research. The implementations, as seen in [86, 219], used a fixed-size window and weighting functions to capture the spatial neighbourhood of a pixel. This information was then integrated into the JSRC model for classification. Even superpixel approaches, which rely on segmentation algorithms for contextual information, have successfully utilized JSRC to exploit the extracted spatial information [120, 220, 224]. Furthermore, JSRC can be adapted to incorporate multiscale and multifeature spatial information with only slight modifications, making it a highly versatile model [56, 63].

Dictionary Learning (DL)

An overcomplete dictionary D, which enables sparse representations of pixels in HSI, can either be selected as a predefined set of functions or constructed by adjusting its content to match a given set of pixels. Choosing a predefined matrix (e.g. training samples) is appealing because it is simpler, and it may also lead to simpler and fast algorithms for evaluating the sparse representation. But, as mentioned, the success of such dictionaries in applications depends on how suitable they are to properly describe the unknown pixels for classification. In many cases, the dictionary may not have enough information and hence it may be required to add more atoms into the dictionary to improve classification performance. But in doing so, the size of the dictionary will increase, leading to an increase in the labelling cost and computational burden. Thus, research on learning a quality dictionary is initiated with the objective to find a compact, discriminative and representative dictionary. One such dictionary learning technique is called K-singular value decomposition (K-SVD).

K-SVD was introduced by [1] to learn a dictionary for filling in missing pixels and compression of image. Since then, it has been used for a wide variety of applications. The aim of K-SVD is to learn a compact sized dictionary from given training samples while maintaining the representational power of the dictionary. To do this, K-SVD focuses on minimizing the following reconstruction error:

$$\{\hat{\mathrm{D}}, \hat{\mathrm{A}}_{\mathrm{Z}}\} = \arg\min_{\mathrm{D},\mathrm{A}_{\mathrm{Z}}} \|\mathrm{Z} - \mathrm{D}\mathrm{A}_{\mathrm{Z}}\|_F^2 \quad s.t \ \|\alpha_j\|_0 < K, j = 1, 2, \ldots, M \tag{1.21}$$

where, $\mathrm{Z} = [z_1, z_2, \ldots, z_M]$ are the training samples, D and A_{Z} is a dictionary to be learned and the sparse coefficients of Z respectively. To solve the above optimization problem, the K-SVD algorithm follows a two-step iterative process: (i) sparse coding and (ii) dictionary update. In the sparse coding step, the sparse representation of Z is computed using the dictionary D to produce the sparse matrix $\hat{\mathrm{A}}_{\mathrm{Z}}$. The dictionary update step updates each atom in D at a time using SVD to improve the target function in Eqn. (1.21).

In greater detail, during the sparse coding stage, a fixed dictionary, D, is used to compute sparse coefficients, α_z, for each training sample z using any pursuit algorithm.

$$\hat{\alpha}_z = \arg\min_{\alpha_z} \|z - \mathrm{D}\alpha_z\|_2 \quad s.t \quad \|\alpha_z\|_0 < K \tag{1.22}$$

In the dictionary stage, both the training samples Z and D are fixed. Each dictionary atom d_k is then updated sequentially. This involves identifying a group of training samples that utilize d_k as, $\omega_k = \{i | 1 \leq i \leq Z, \alpha_j^k(i) \neq 0\}$ and calculating the overall representation error, $\mathrm{E_k}$ as

$$\mathrm{E_k} = \mathrm{Z} - \sum_{j \neq k} d_j \alpha_j^{train} \tag{1.23}$$

To focus on relevant information, $\mathrm{E_k}$ is restricted to $\mathrm{E_k^R}$ by selecting only the atoms associated with the current group of training samples ω_k. Finally, SVD is applied to $\mathrm{E_k^R}$ to decompose it into the matrices U, Σ and V such that $\mathrm{E_k^R} = \mathrm{U\Sigma V^T}$. The first column of the left singular vector matrix U is then utilized to update the dictionary atom d_k while the first column of the right singular vector matrix V, scaled by the singular value $\Sigma(1,1)$ is used to update the sparse coefficients α_{ω_k}. This iterative process continues for all dictionary atoms until convergence is achieved.

However, K-SVD primarily emphasizes the representational capability of the dictionary while neglecting its discriminative ability. To overcome this limitation, several of its variants are proposed in the literature that produce a dictionary with better discrimination power [103, 267]. Besides using K-SVD, several authors developed dictionary learning (DL) methods such as FDDL[252], LSDDL [75], class-wise DL [82], that produce discriminative dictionaries by embedding interclass and intraclass information into the objective function. Recently, researchers have focused on incorporating spatial information into the dictionary learning process to enhance the HSI classification performance [145, 202, 224, 240].

1.3 Objectives

The rich spectral information of HSI has found to be useful for classification of various land cover types and objects. But developing a robust technique for this purpose is still considered a challenging task. While sparse representation has proven itself to be a powerful technique, it still has some issues in effectively and accurately classifying the HSI. Therefore, the objective of this thesis is to *develop advanced techniques for HSI classification by exploiting sparse representation clas-*

sifier. This objective is achieved through the following four specific goals.

1. *To develop a spectral-spatial sparse representation based method that incorporates better spatial contextual information for the classification of hyperspectral images.* To incorporate the spatial contextual information of the pixel, existing spectral-spatial methods rely on fixed-size windows or superpixels. However, the inability to simultaneously consider the appropriate spatial neighbourhoods and correlated information even at different scales limits their performance. This goal of the research aims to define a new strategy that models better contextual information and mitigates the drawbacks of existing methods.

2. *To develop a robust dictionary learning method that exploits spectral-spatial information for hyperspectral image classification.* Several dictionary learning techniques have effectively improved the sparse representation model's ability to classify the HSI. Some of them use only spectral information, while others use spectral-spatial information. However, their level of effectiveness is dependent on the discriminative power of this spectral or spectral-spatial information used to learn the dictionary. Therefore, the goal of this research is to develop a robust method that extracts better spectral-spatial information from HSI and use it to build a dictionary learning process that enhance the classification performance.

3. *To develop a novel spectral-spatial feature set for hyperspectral image classification.* The advancement of spectral-spatial features has been instrumental in improving the performance of HSI classification. Their aim is to extract better features by mitigating the effect of noisy pixels while simultaneously emphasizing relevant spatial information through local spatial relationships of each pixel. However, the inherent high dimensionality and complexity of HSI make this task an ongoing challenge to overcome. The goal of this research is to develop a novel spectral-spatial feature set that captures richer spectral-spatial information, improving both discrimination and representa-

tion capabilities for enhanced classification performance.

4. *To develop an active learning model for hyperspectral image classification using sparse representation classifier.* In many HSI applications, acquiring labelled samples is both time-consuming and expensive. Active learning is a framework that minimizes labeling efforts while enhancing classifier performance by selecting only the most informative samples for the training set. Although the sparse representation classifier (SRC) has already proven to be a robust classifier and has been successfully used in many applications, it is seldom used jointly with AL. This goal of the research is to define an AL query function containing both uncertainty and diversity criteria by exploiting the properties of the SRC in kernel space for better selection of informative samples.

1.4 Organization of the thesis

The thesis is organized as follows:

Chapter 1 introduces the concept of HSI and describes the different challenges of its classification. It also discusses several approaches that provide solutions to the above challenges, such as incorporation of spatial information, dimensionality reduction, and active learning. And finally, list out the objectives of the thesis.

Chapter 2 presents a novel method that constructs modified max-tree and min-tree to represent the connected components of the image for better modelling of the spatial contextual information. The proposed method then exploit these connected components to define adaptive multiscale windows that determine the appropriate spatial neighbourhoods of the pixels in HSI. Finally, the multiscale spatial neighbourhoods of the pixels are fed into a sparse classification model to classify the HSI [14, 17]. Experiments conducted on three real datasets show that our technique achieved better classification accuracy than other similar existing techniques.

Chapter 3 presents a novel dictionary learning method for the classification of HSI. In contrast to the previous approach, the method propose a simple and computationally efficient technique to define spatial neighbourhoods of the pixels. The method first uses superpixels and a fixed window to identify the appropriate spatial neighbourhoods of the pixel. Then, taking each spatial contextual information within these neighbourhood, SVD is applied to extract the context-sensitive spectral features (CSSF) of it. Thus, for a pixel, multiple CSSFs are extracted by considering its spatial neighbourhoods at different scales. Then, for each CSSF, a dictionary is learned by adopting the DKSVD dictionary learning algorithm. Finally, the classification results provided by the individual dictionary are ensembles to predict the final result. The experiments were conducted on three real hyperspectral datsets and the results show the effectiveness of the proposed method.

Chapter 4 presents a novel method for extracting novel spectral-spatial features in HSI. In contrast to the first and second approaches, here multiple fixed window of increasing size are used to define spatial neighbourhoods of the pixel. The method first reduces the dimensionality of the HSI by PCA. Then it exploits SVD to obtain the rank-1 approximation of the pixels inside a fixed-size window. The features associated to the center pixel of the window, called rank-1 spectral-spatial features (RSSF) are then used to represent the pixel. To capture proper spatial contextual information, multiple windows of increasing size are considered for each pixel, resulting in the generation of multiple RSSFs. These RSSFs are stacked together to form a Multiscale RSSF (MRSSF). Finally, the pixels represented with their MRSSF are fed into a sparse classification model to classify the HSI. The experiments carried out on four real benchmark hyperspectral datasets demonstrate the effectiveness of the proposed method.

Chapter 5 presents two novel active learning (AL) methods for the classification of HSI. The first method uses only a single spectral feature, while the second method uses a multifeature concept to define the query function. The proposed query functions include uncertainty and diversity criteria, both of which are defined by exploiting the kernel sparse representation classifier (KSRC) [15, 16]. Experiments conducted using three datasets show that the proposed methods provides significantly better classification results compared to many popular state-of-the-art AL methods.

Chapter 6 serves as the conclusion of this thesis. It provides a summary of the research conducted, highlighting key findings and contributions, and also outlined potential future directions in this area.

Chapter 2

Component Adaptive Sparse Representation for Hyperspectral Image Classification

2.1 Introduction

As learned from the previous chapter, each pixel in the image is classified according to its spectral values in pixel-wise HSI classification. However, due to the noisy nature of the image caused by low spatial resolution and other environmental factors, these classification techniques often produce misclassified maps. Sparse Representation Classification (SRC), being a pixel-wise technique, is also susceptible to these limitations. Consequently, several methods have been proposed in the literature that integrate both spectral and spatial information to mitigate these challenges and improve classification performance. These methods used single or multiple windows to extract the contextual information and, after which, it is incorporated into the sparse classifier for classification.

In the literature, fixed-size windows or superpixels are used to define these windows. But on one hand, the fixed-size windows would not be able to define the actual spatial neighbourhood of the pixels. And, on the other hand, the shapes and sizes of the windows determined by superpixels are dependent on the segmentation techniques. Thus, the development of robust methods to define an appropriate spatial neighbourhood is still a challenging and relevant research topic. To mitigate the limitations of the existing models, this chapter introduces a novel approach that exploits the connected components of the image to define an improved spatial neighborhood for each unlabelled pixel. To this end, we propose a novel technique for constructing modified max-trees and min-trees to represent different connected components of the image based on the predefined threshold value for filtering. It is important to note that, in contrast to conventional max-tree and min-tree based attribute filtering [187], the proposed technique merges all connected components with attribute values below the specified threshold. The filter images resulting from both the modified max-tree and min-tree, generated using multiple thresholds, are then utilized as reference images. Finally, we present a novel method that automatically defines the shape of windows to represent the spatial neighbourhood of each unlabelled pixel by looking at the surrounding connected components present in the reference images. Since the windows corresponding to an unlabelled pixel are determined by looking into the connected components surrounding it, their size and shape are adaptive, allowing them to retain neighboring pixels within the same homogeneous region. This enables the capture of maximum spatial contextual information with few multi-scale windows. As a result, by defining these windows based on connected components of the image, the limitations of existing techniques are effectively mitigated. Note that in the past, several authors have used connected components to generate attribute profiles for the spectral-spatial classification of HSI [11, 39, 42, 133]. Some researchers used this profile to train sparse representation classifiers [79, 96, 200]. But no one exploited connected components to define adaptive windows for incorporating the spatial neighbourhood of a pixel.

The organization of this chapter is as follows. Section 2.2 presents the proposed component adaptive sparse representation classification model in detail. The experimental results and analysis are reported in Section 2.3. Finally, Section 2.4 gives the concluding remarks.

2.2 Proposed Method

As mentioned above, the existing techniques have certain drawbacks arising from the use of fixed-size square windows or their reliability on the segmentation algorithms that hinders the effective capture of spatial information. In this research, a novel technique was proposed that defines component adaptive multiscale windows to represent spatial neighbourhoods of each pixel by analysing the connected components of the image.The entire framework of our proposed technique is depicted in Figure 2-1. Our method involves constructing modified max-trees and min-trees based on a predefined threshold to represent different connected components. These modified trees are used to generate filtered images across multiple thresholds, and the resulting connected components are analyzed to define adaptive multiscale windows for each unlabelled pixel's spatial neighborhood. Finally, the spatial neighbourhoods represented by these windows are used for classification. The detailed description of different steps of the proposed technique is given below.

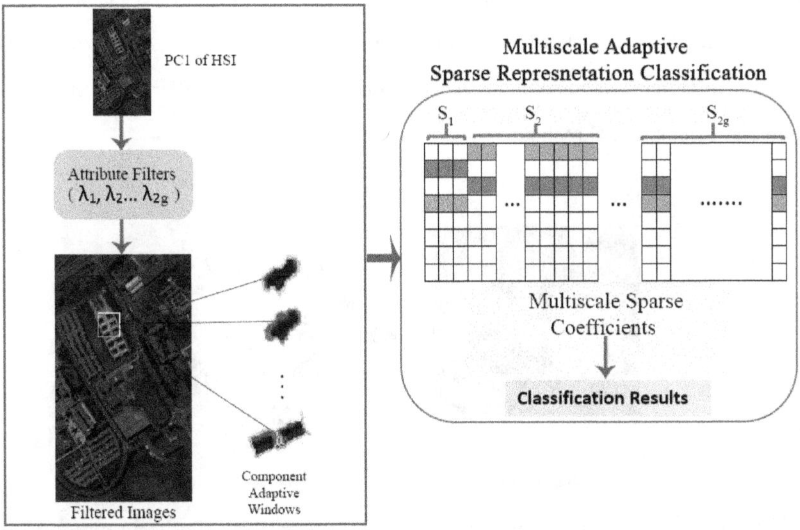

Figure 2-1: Illustration of the framework of the proposed method.

2.2.1 Proposed Attribute Filtering

As observed from the previous chapter, attribute filtering (AF) is a widely used approach for analysing the spatial information of an image. It creates a filtered image by following three steps: tree construction, filtering, and image generation [187]. In the literature, the connected components of an input image are most commonly represented using max-tree and min-tree structures. [26, 43]. However, the filtered images generated from these trees often contain many small connected components whose attribute values are below a certain threshold. Hence, this makes them unsuitable for defining proper spatial neighbourhoods. Figure 2-2 shows a toy image and its corresponding max-tree representation. From this figure, one can see that the node N_1^2 represents two connected components $B1$ and $C1$. During filtering, it is not possible to filter them individually, as the same node represents them. As a result, they will not be merged with their parents even if their individual attribute value is less than the considered threshold value. The same problem also persists for the min-tree representation. In order to overcome these challenges, a novel technique was proposed that combines tree construction and filtering steps together to generate a modified max-tree (min-tree) where each node of the tree represents connected components that have higher attribute values than the predefined threshold.

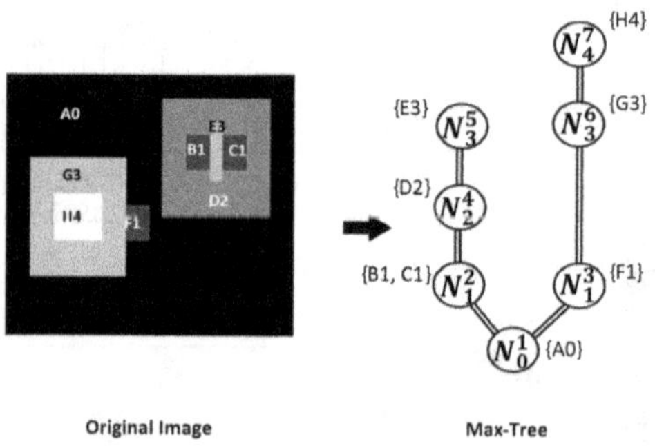

Figure 2-2: Max-tree constructed by the conventional method represents different connected components of the input image

The proposed filtering technique first constructs the modified max-tree (min-

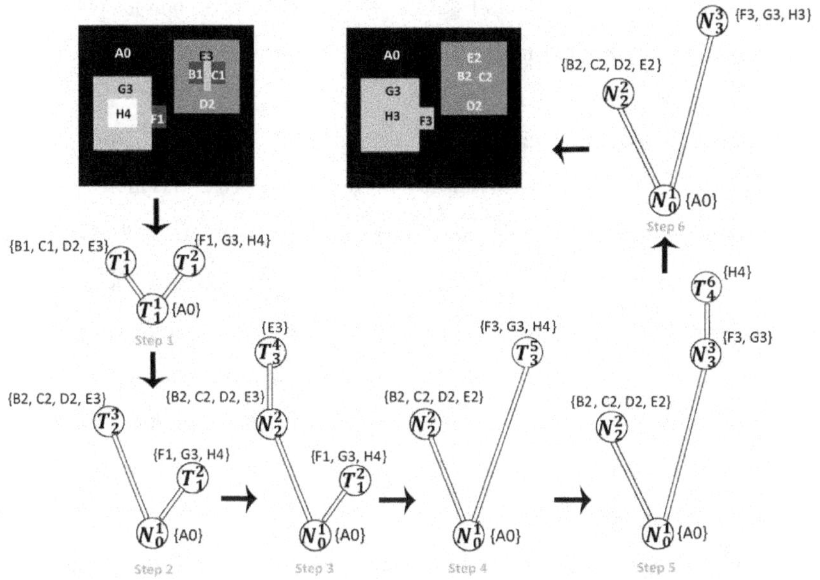

Figure 2-3: Construction of the proposed max-tree and the filter image obtained from it

tree) by combining tree construction and filtering steps of the conventional AF. Then, the image restitution step of the conventional filtering is used to generate the filter image from the constructed modified max-tree (min-tree). In contrast to the conventional max-tree (min-tree) construction that uses only a two-fold procedure based on a *binarization step* and a *connected component definition step*, the proposed technique adds a filtering process, called *merging step*, thus turning the max-tree (min-tree) construction phase into a three-fold procedure. Firstly, the *binarization step* splits the image into 'local background set' and 'local background complement set'. Secondly, the *merging step* finds the connected components from the local background set, whose attribute values do not satisfy the predefined criterion and then merges them to their neighbour connected component having the next higher gray value. Thus, the merging step moves some connected components (whose attribute values do not satisfy the criterion) from local background set to local background complement set. Finally, in the *connected component definition step*, the connected components from the local background complement set are analysed to form the child nodes. The three steps are recursively reiterated for each child node to build the final tree.

In greater detail, Figure 2-3, visually depicts the steps of the proposed filtering technique using a simplified toy image. It can be seen that the image contains many connected components denoted by alphabet {A, B, C, D, E, F, G, H} followed by a number {0, 1, 2, 3, 4} representing the gray value of the connected components. To generate the filter image, here we consider *area* as the attribute and the filtering criterion *'area of the connected component greater than threshold* $\lambda = 20$ *pixels'*. Let us assume that the areas of the connected components B1, C1, E3, F1 and H4 are below 20 pixels. The proposed technique first constructs a modified max-tree (min-tree) to generate the filter image. Initially, the minimum gray value 0 is considered as threshold value ($v_g = 0$) for binarization and the binarization step generates the local background set {A0} (pixels with v_g gray value) as well as the local background complement set {B1, C1, D2, E3, F1, G3, H4} (pixels with $> v_g$ gray value). After that, the merging step processes the temporary node $T_0^1 = \{A0\}$ that represents the local background set. Since $area(A0) > 20$, the merging step converts T_0^1 into the permanent node $N_0^1 = A0$. Then the connected component definition step analyses the connected components present in the local background complement set and generates two child nodes $T_1^1 = \{B1, C1, D2, E3\}$ and $T_1^2 = \{F1, G3, H4\}$. Next, the same three-fold steps are applied by considering the pixels in T_1^1 as input image and the threshold $v_g = 1$ for binarization. This time the binarization step generates the local background set {B1, C1} and the local background complement set {D2, E3}. The merging step involves computing the attribute values of the connected components within the local background set. Since $area(B1) < 20$ and $area(C1) < 20$, both the connected components B1 and C1 are merged to the next higher connected component present in local background complement set (i.e. D2) and the node T_1^1 is removed. Then, the connected component definition step creates a temporary node $T_2^3 = \{B2, C2, D2, E3\}$ to represent the connected components present in the local background complement set. Now, considering the pixels in T_2^3 as input image, the three-fold steps are applied for $v_g = 2$. The binarization step generates the local background set {B2, C2, D2} and local background complement set {E3}. In the merging step T_2^3 is converted to permanent node $N_2^2 = \{B2, C2, D2\}$ as $area(B2, C2, D2) > 20$. The connected component definition step creates a temporary node $T_3^4 = \{E3\}$ and then merged it with its parent node $N_2^2 = \{B2, C2, D2, E2\}$ as $area(E3) < 20$. The same process is recursively applied to construct the final modified max-tree, as shown in step 6 of Figure 2-3. Similar to the modified max-tree, the modified min-tree is constructed by processing the connected components from brighter to darker pixels. Figure 2-4 shows the modified min-tree constructed from the considered toy image for the *area* attribute with threshold $\lambda = 20$.

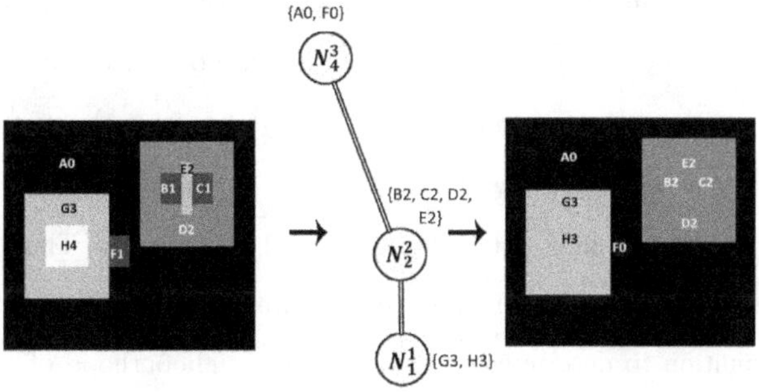

Figure 2-4: Filter image obtained from the proposed min-tree

Once the proposed max-tree (min-tree) is constructed, it is used to restore the gray scale image as filter image. In this image, the attribute values of all connected components are higher than the threshold λ. Figure 2-3 and Figure 2-4 show the filter image obtained from the modified max-tree and modified min-tree, respectively, constructed using *area* attribute with threshold $\lambda = 20$. From these figures, one can see that all the connected components of the original image whose attribute values are smaller than the predefined threshold (i.e., $\lambda = 20$) are merged to their neighbour connected components. Moreover, the spatial information capture by the filter image generated from modified max-tree is different from the one obtained using modified min-tree, as they merge the uncertain connected components (e.g. F1) into different neighbour components.

2.2.2 Component Adaptive Multiscale Windows

In order to define the spatial neighbourhood for each unlabelled pixel within the HSI, the proposed technique exploits the image's connected components. To achieve this, the first principal component (PC) of the HSI is computed. Subsequently, this principal component serves as the input for the construction of modified max-trees and min-trees using a range of thresholds, resulting in the generation of multiple filtered images. In this work, we use the *area* attribute and g threshold values with increasing order ($i.e., \lambda_1 < \lambda_2, ..., < \lambda_g$) to generate g modified max-tree and g modified min-tree. As a result, $2g$ filter images containing connected components having different sizes are obtained. Since, *area* is an increasing attribute, the filter image generated (either from the max-tree, or the min-tree) by considering a large threshold value contains larger connected components by merging smaller neighbour connected components. Thus, the sizes of the connected components in the filter images are adaptive in nature and provide useful information to determine the appropriate neighbourhood of each pixel in the image. Since, the number of generated filter images is $2g$, each pixel of the HSI is associated with $2g$ connected components (one from each filter image). To represent spatial neighbourhood for an unlabelled pixel y, the size, and shape of the $2g$ connected components associated with the pixel y are considered to define $2g$ windows.

Figure 2-5 shows the component adaptive multiscale windows obtained by the proposed technique using the 1st PC on the University of Pavia dataset. To represent spatial neighbourhoods of a pixel, four windows of different sizes are defined by generating 4 filter images using *area* attribute with two thresholds

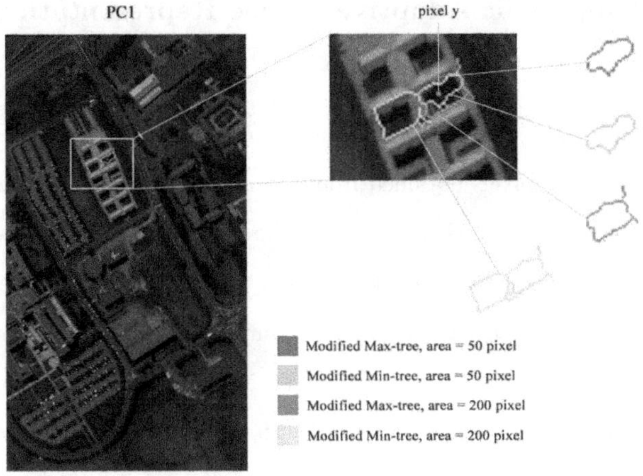

Figure 2-5: Component adaptive multiscale windows define by the proposed technique for a pixel **y**

($\lambda_1 = 50, \lambda_2 = 200$). The pixel y is associated with four connected components (one from each filter image) and the sizes of these connected components used to define the windows are shown in different colours. The windows depicted in dark blue and light blue are derived from the connected components of the filter image generated by the modified max-tree and modified min-tree, respectively, using a threshold parameter of $\lambda_1 = 50$. Similarly, the red and green windows originate from the connected components of the filter image produced by the modified max-tree and modified min-tree, respectively, with a threshold of $\lambda_2 = 200$. These four-scale component-adaptive windows, obtained through the proposed technique, are subsequently used to define the spatial neighborhoods of pixel y. From the figure, it can be observed that the size and shape of the object to which the pixel belong to is retained by the windows. Some windows expand their sizes to include other similar objects (as seen from the green window) by keeping the heterogeneity inside the window to a minimum. Therefore, the proposed component adaptive multiscale window defines adaptive and homogeneous spatial neighbourhoods, thus leading to better modelling of spatial information. This information is then used for classification, as describes in the next section.

2.2.3 Component Adaptive Sparse Representation Classification (CASRC)

The final step of the proposed technique is to classify each unlabelled pixel by including neighbour pixels obtained from the corresponding multiscale windows defined by the proposed technique. Since the connected components of the filter images determine the size of the windows, there is a good chance of getting some large windows with lots of similar (redundant) neighbour pixels. As a result, the classification process becomes time-consuming. To mitigate this issue, we apply a smart sampling strategy to select few pixels from the windows, whose sizes are larger than a predefined threshold O. Our sampling strategy randomly samples a high percentage of neighbour pixels that are close to the observed unlabelled pixel, and gradually decreases the percentage of sampling as the distance from it increases. Once the sampling is over, the selected neighbour pixels within each window are stored in a multiscale matrix $\mathrm{Y}^{\mathrm{Multiscale}} = [\mathrm{Y}^1, \mathrm{Y}^2, ..., \mathrm{Y}^{2\mathrm{g}}]$, where $Y^i, (i \in 1, 2, .., 2g)$ consists of pixels sampled from the spatial neighbourhood defined by the ith window. Then the multiscale matrix is used for classification of the corresponding unlabelled pixels. In this chapter, we use the same sparse representation based classifier as proposed in MASRC [56] for its ability to exploit correlation between the information from each spatial neighbourhood.

For a HSI $\mathbf{H}$ of B bands, the spectral signature of each pixel is captured by a $B \times 1$ column vector, where each element corresponds to the intensity value in a specific band. Suppose that the image $\mathbf{H}$ has C distinct classes and N training pixels. Let D_i be the training pixels of ith class and N_i be the number of pixels in D_i. Then, the dictionary $\mathrm{D} = [\mathrm{D}_1, \mathrm{D}_2, ..., \mathrm{D}_\mathrm{C}]$ is a $B \times N$ matrix containing N training pixels such that $N = \sum_{i=1}^{C} N_i$. After computing the 1st PC from $\mathbf{H}$, the $2g$ filter images, $\mathrm{R} = [\mathrm{R}_{\lambda_1}^{\max}, \mathrm{R}_{\lambda_1}^{\min}, \mathrm{R}_{\lambda_2}^{\max}, \mathrm{R}_{\lambda_2}^{\min}, ..., \mathrm{R}_{\lambda_\mathrm{g}}^{\max}, \mathrm{R}_{\lambda_\mathrm{g}}^{\min}]$ are generated by applying the proposed filtering technique using *area* attribute and g thresholds $\lambda_1 < \lambda_2 < ..., < \lambda_g$. Then, for an unlabelled pixel $y \in \mathbf{H}$, by analysing filtered images in R, the proposed technique defines $2g$ component adaptive windows to represent spatial neighbourhoods of y. After performing the smart sampling, the pixels from each spatial neighbourhood are stored in a multiscale matrix $\mathrm{Y}^{\mathrm{Multiscale}} = [\mathrm{Y}^1, \mathrm{Y}^2, ..., \mathrm{Y}^{2\mathrm{g}}]$. The multiscale matrix $\mathrm{Y}^{\mathrm{Multiscale}}$ can be expressed as:

$$\mathrm{Y}^{\mathrm{Multiscale}} = \mathrm{D}\mathrm{A}^{\mathrm{Multiscale}} \tag{2.1}$$

Now using the dictionary D, the multiscale sparse representation $\mathrm{A}^{\mathrm{Multiscale}}$ can be determined by solving the subsequent optimization problem.

$$\hat{\mathrm{A}}^{\mathrm{Multiscale}} = \underset{\mathrm{A}^{\mathrm{Multiscale}}}{\arg\min} \|\mathrm{Y}^{\mathrm{Multiscale}} - \mathrm{D}\mathrm{A}^{\mathrm{Multiscale}}\|_{\mathrm{F}} \tag{2.2}$$

subject to $\|\mathrm{A}^{\mathrm{Multiscale}}\|_{adaptive,0} < K$

Here, K represents sparsity level, $\|.\|_F$ is the Frobenius norm and $\|\mathrm{A}^{\mathrm{Multiscale}}\|_{adaptive,0}$ represents the number of sparse coefficients in each scale. The optimization problem in (2.2) can be solved using the algorithm presented in [56]. After the multiscale sparse representation is recovered, the class label $\hat{c}$ for the unlabelled sample y is computed as follows:

$$\hat{c} = \arg\min_{i} \|\mathrm{Y}^{\mathrm{Multiscale}} - \mathrm{D_i}\hat{\mathrm{A}}_{\mathrm{i}}^{\mathrm{Multiscale}}\|_F \quad i \in 1, 2, 3, .., C \tag{2.3}$$

where $\hat{\mathrm{A}}_i^{Multiscale}$ represents the sparse coefficient of $\mathrm{D_i}$.

In our proposed work, the time complexity for the construction of modified max-tree (min-tree) is $\mathcal{O}(Tv_g)$, where T denotes the number of pixels in total and v_g is the height of the tree. After tree construction, the computational complexity associated with the classification process is $\mathcal{O}(TNKp)$, with N being the number of dictionary atoms, K the sparsity level and p the number of pixels in the maximal window size. Algorithm 2 shows a summary of the steps of the proposed method.

Algorithm 2 Proposed CASRC

Input: Hyperspectral Image $\mathbf{H}$; sparsity level K; Dictionary D; attribute thresholds $(\lambda_1, \lambda_2, ...\lambda_g)$.

```
Compute PC1 from H.
Generate filter images, R = [R^max_λ1, R^min_λ1, R^max_λ2, R^min_λ2, ..., R^max_λg, R^min_λg] using modified max-tree and modified min-tree.
for each unlabelled pixel y do
    Define 2g component adaptive multiscale windows w_i, i = 1, 2, ..., 2g using the proposed technique.
    for i = 1 to 2g do
        if sizeof(w_i) > O then
            w_i = smart_sampling_strategy(w_i)
        end if
        Y^i = w_i
    end for
    Y^Multiscale = [Y^1, Y^2, ..., Y^2g]
    Compute Â^Multiscale by solving Equation (2.2)
    Compute ĉ using Equation (2.3)
    Assign ĉ as the class label of y
end for
```

2.3 Experimental Results

The experimental design and the results acquired by the proposed technique are described in this section.

2.3.1 Experimental Setup

In order to assess the proposed technique's effectiveness, widely recognized hyperspectral datasets – namely, University of Pavia, Indian Pines and University of Houston 2013 are used. The description of each of these datasets is given in Appendix A. The performance of our proposed technique was compared against other state-of-the-art sparse representation-based methods that incorporate spatial information by exploiting neighboring pixels. The five existing techniques considered are the SRC [28], JSRC [29],MSSRC [268], the MASRC[56] and the DSDL [224]. In this experiment, the proposed technique used four thresholds $\lambda_1 = 30, \lambda_2 = 100, \lambda_3 = 200$, and $\lambda_4 = 300$ to generate eight filter images for all the considered datasets. The threshold used for smart sampling is fixed as $O = 300$

while the number of sparsity is fixed as $K = 3$. Among the five literature methods, the SRC technique does not use contextual information. The JSRC technique uses a fixed-size single window to incorporate spatial information. In this experiment, for all the three datasets, the window size for JSRC is fixed as 5×5. In the MSSRC and DSDL technique, multiple windows are defined to incorporate spatial information. The size of each adaptive window or superpixel relies on the number of segments n and is defined as $n = T/n_{sup}$, with T denoting the number of pixels in total and n_{sup} is the number of pixels in each superpixel. Clearly n is varied for different datasets. In this experiment, for the MASRC algorithm, seven square shape windows of different scales $[3 \times 3, 5 \times 5, 7 \times 7, 9 \times 9, 11 \times 11, 13 \times 13, 15 \times 15]$ are used. The sparsity level for all the techniques is fixed as $K = 3$. Table 2.1 shows the parameters of the different methods and their values considered for the experiment.

Table 2.1: Parameters of the different methods and their values considered for the experiment

Sl No.	Method	Parameters	
		Thresholds(Windows)	Sparsity (K)
1	SRC	–	3
2	JSRC	5×5	3
3	MSSRC	$n_i = T/n_{sup}$	3
4	MASRC	$3 \times 3 \ldots 15 \times 15$	3
5	DSDL	$n_i = N_{sup}/n_{sup}$	3
6	CASRC	$\lambda_i = 30, 100, 200, 300$	3

All experiments related to the implementation of the proposed technique and the comparative state-of-the-art methods were conducted within the Matlab environment. The computational platform consisted of a desktop system running a 64-bit Operating System, equipped with Intel(R) Core(TM) i5-10500 CPU at 3.10GHz processing power and 24 GB RAM.

2.3.2 Results

Across all considered datasets, the effectiveness of the proposed method was evaluated through two distinct sets of experiments. For the first set of experiments,

Table 2.2: Training and testing samples for the University of Pavia, Indian Pines, and University of Houston 2013 datasets.

University of Pavia			Indian Pines			University of Houston 2013		
Name	Training Sample	Testing Sample	Name	Training Sample	Testing Sample	Name	Training Sample	Testing Sample
Asphalt	300	6331	Alfalfa	5	41	Grass Healthy	126	1125
Meadows	300	18349	Corn-Notill	143	1285	Grass Stresses	126	1128
Gravel	300	1799	Corn-Mintill	83	747	Grass Synthetic	70	627
Broad Trees	300	2764	Corn	24	213	Tree	125	1119
PMS	300	1045	Grass-Pasture	48	435	Soil	125	1119
Bare Soil	300	4729	Grass-Trees	73	657	Water	33	292
Bitumen	300	1030	Grs-Pas-Mow	3	25	Residential	127	1141
SBB	300	3382	Hay-Windrowed	48	430	Commercial	125	1119
Shadows	300	647	Oats	2	18	Road	126	1126
			Soyabean-Notill	97	875	Highway	123	1104
			Soyabean-Mintill	246	2209	Railway	124	1111
			Soyabean Clean	59	534	Parking Lot 1	124	1109
			Wheat	21	184	Parking Lot 2	47	422
			Woods	127	1138	Tennis Court	43	385
			B-G-T-D	40	347	Running Track	66	594
			Stone-Steel-Towers	9	84			

two sampling strategies were initially evaluated for selecting training and testing sample. One is a stratified sampling strategy, whereby a balanced representation of samples from each class are selected for training and the rest are used for testing and a spatially constrained sampling strategy, whereby samples are drawn from separate local regions. However since both provided similar results, stratified sampling strategy was chosen for this first experiment. This experiment helped to assess the stability of the different techniques for a variety of training and test sets. Table 2.2 shows the different number of training and testing samples for each dataset. The second set of experiments used standard (fixed) training and test sets created by the remote sensing community, as reported in [69]. In the experiment, three quantitative metrics are used to evaluate each technique: Overall Accuracy (OA), Average Accuracy (AA) and Kappa (κ). The OA measures the number of pixels that are classified correctly. The AA measures the number of pixels that are correctly classified in each class and κ measures the *degree of agreement* of the classifier.

Table 2.3: Classification results obtained by the TCSRC and CASRC for all the considered datasets.

Experiment 1: Randomly Chosen Training and Test Sets (five runs)						
Dataset	**TCSRC**			**Proposed CASRC**		
	$\overline{OA}$	$\overline{AA}$	$\overline{\kappa}$	$\overline{OA}$	$\overline{AA}$	$\overline{\kappa}$
Pavia	89.86 ±0.20	87.33 ±0.37	0.83±0.00	**99.00** ±0.25	**98.75** ±0.21	**0.99**±0.00
Indian Pine	76.64 ±0.37	73.30 ±1.19	0.73±0.01	**97.97** ±0.26	**96.51** ±0.42	**0.98** ±0.00
Houston	93.52 ±0.17	92.55 ±0.21	0.93±0.00	**97.6** ±0.51	**97.45** ±0.58	**0.97** ±0.00
Experiment 2: Standard Training and Test Sets						
Dataset	**TCSRC**			**Proposed CASRC**		
	OA	AA	κ	OA	AA	κ
Pavia	72.79	80.38	0.65	**81.11**	**84.70**	**0.75**
Indian Pine	69.02	77.12	0.65	**96.29**	**97.55**	**0.96**
Houston	75.03	79.02	0.73	**78.29**	**81.07**	**0.77**

Existing Max-tree (Min-tree) vs Proposed Max-tree (Min-tree)

As mentioned above, filter images generated using traditional max-trees (min-trees) may contain numerous connected components with attribute values below the specified threshold, making them not suitable for defining appropriate spatial neighborhoods. To address this limitation, this work introduces a modified max-tree (min-tree) construction. To demonstrate its potential, classification results obtained with our technique are compared to those using the existing max-tree (min-tree). We named it Traditional Component Sparse Representation Classification (TCSRC) for future reference. Table 2.3 reports the classification results obtained by both the proposed CASRC and the TCSRC techniques using the same parameters. From the table one can see that for all the three datasets, the classification results obtained by using the proposed max-tree (min-tree) are much better than the existing max-tree (min-tree). For Indian Pines datasets, the proposed max-tree (min-tree) improves the classification results more than 20% as compared to the existing one. This shows the robustness of the proposed max-tree (min-tree) for defining better spatial neighbourhoods.

Table 2.4: Classification results obtained by the SRC [28], the JSRC [29], the MSSRC [268], the MASRC[56], DSDL [224] and proposed CASRC (University of Pavia dataset).

	Experiment 1: Randomly Chosen Training and Test Sets (five runs)					
Class Name	**SRC**	**JSRC**	**MSSRC**	**MASRC**	**DSDL**	**Proposed CASRC**
Asphalt	63.45	71.44	94.34	94.07	96.22	97.92
Meadow	81.94	93.49	99.43	99.39	99.71	99.26
Gravel	70.51	97.23	99.91	100.00	99.91	99.97
Tree	92.23	96.79	97.43	98.10	98.26	96.02
Metal Sheet	99.75	99.94	99.61	100.00	99.75	99.96
Bare Soil	71.05	92.88	99.98	99.96	99.98	99.96
Bitumen	87.44	99.73	100.00	100.00	99.98	99.94
Brick	72.85	92.41	98.24	99.41	99.72	99.34
Shadow	98.30	93.97	81.91	92.89	78.95	95.86
$\overline{OA}$	78.03 ±0.49	90.57 ±0.62	98.21 ±0.30	98.48 ±0.23	98.77 ±0.52	**99.00** ±0.25
$\overline{AA}$	81.95 ±0.46	93.09 ±0.10	96.76 ±0.53	98.20 ±0.12	96.94 ±0.51	**98.75** ±0.21
$\overline{\kappa}$	0.71 ±0.01	0.87 ±0.01	0.98 ±0.00	0.98 ±0.00	0.98 ±0.00	**0.99** ±0.00
	Experiment 2: Standard Training and Test Sets					
OA	69.05	71.57	77.83	76.04	75.71	**81.11**
AA	76.77	76.38	77.54	80.94	80.38	**85.28**
κ	0.61	0.63	0.66	0.69	0.69	**0.75**

University of Pavia Dataset

For the first experiment conducted on the University of Pavia dataset, 300 labelled samples from each class are randomly selected for training and the rest are used for testing. This experimental procedure was repeated five times, and the average classification results achieved by various techniques were computed. Table 2.4 shows the average accuracies obtained by SRC, JSRC, MSSRC, MASRC, DSDL and the proposed CASRC techniques. From this table, one can see that our CASRC technique provides better results compared to all the five state-of-the-art techniques. For qualitative analysis, Figure 2-6 displays the classification maps generated by the different techniques.

In the second experiment, the standard training and test sets of the University of Pavia dataset are used for comparison. Table 2.4 also reports the classification accuracies obtained by the different techniques using this standard training and test sets. From the table, one can see that there is a sharp improvement in the overall and average accuracy. The proposed technique has an OA of 81.11% and an AA of 84.70% which are both approximately 5% higher than its multiscale

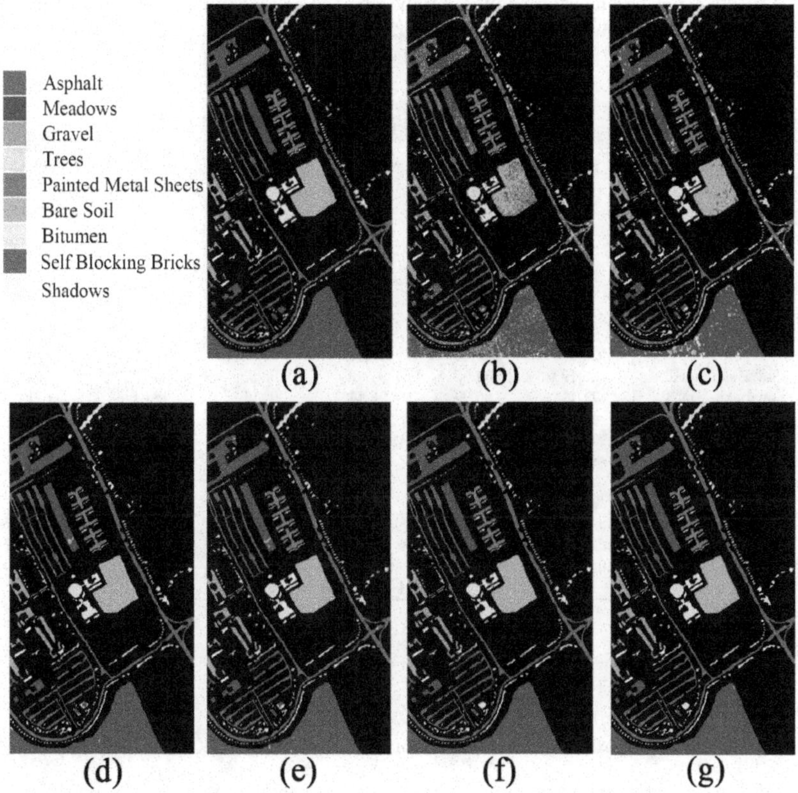

Figure 2-6: University of Pavia dataset: a) Ground truth image. Classification maps generated by b) SRC, c) JSRC, d) MSSRC, e) MASRC, f) DSDL and g) proposed CASRC

counterparts, the MSSRC, MASRC and DSDL techniques. This shows the potentiality of the proposed component adaptive multiscale windows for incorporating spatial information.

Indian Pines Dataset

For the first experiment conducted on the Indian Pines dataset, 10% of labelled samples from each class are randomly selected for training and the rest 90% are used for testing. This experimental procedure was repeated five times again and the average classification results achieved by various techniques were computed.

Table 2.5: Classification results obtained by the SRC [28], the JSRC [29], the MSSRC [268], the MASRC[56], DSDL [224] and the proposed CASRC (Indian Pines dataset).

Experiment 1: Randomly Chosen Training and Test Sets (five runs)						
Class Name	**SRC**	**JSRC**	**MSSRC**	**MASRC**	**DSDL**	**Proposed CASRC**
Alfalfa	46.83	92.20	97.56	94.15	86.34	91.71
Corn-Notill	54.54	93.42	95.88	97.70	96.72	96.03
Corn-Mintill	51.91	93.39	96.28	98.05	96.39	96.84
Corn	36.24	89.30	99.06	96.53	93.15	92.68
Grass-Pasture	83.08	94.16	95.72	96.32	95.59	96.37
Grass-Trees	90.68	97.14	99.85	99.82	99.82	99.42
Grass-Pasture-Mowed	79.20	95.20	36.00	99.20	0.00	92.80
Hay-Windrowed	94.05	99.49	100.00	100.00	100.00	99.95
Oats	26.67	63.33	13.33	73.33	0.00	94.44
Soyabean-Notill	66.19	94.03	91.93	96.55	96.73	97.01
Soyabean-Mintill	71.11	96.99	98.14	99.05	98.81	99.11
Soyabean Clean	43.18	90.52	93.60	97.90	95.51	98.43
Wheat	92.93	94.67	99.46	98.37	99.46	99.46
Woods	88.68	98.93	99.89	100.00	99.81	99.60
B-G-T-D	35.32	83.99	97.57	96.94	99.08	98.50
Stone-Steel-Towers	88.10	92.62	99.52	96.43	95.24	92.62
$\overline{OA}$	68.63 ±0.76	94.94 ±0.63	96.83 ±0.80	**98.32** ±0.31	97.37 ±0.44	97.97 ±0.26
$\overline{AA}$	65.54 ±1.45	91.84 ±0.57	88.36 ±2.83	**96.27** ±0.70	84.53 ±0.92	96.51±0.42
$\overline{\kappa}$	0.64 ±0.01	0.94 ±0.00	0.96 ±0.01	**0.98** ±0.00	0.97 ±0.00	**0.98** ±0.00
Experiment 2: Standard Training and Test Sets						
(OA)	61.08	85.82	93.98	94.43	93.35	**96.29**
(AA)	70.43	92.35	94.97	97.47	96.21	**97.55**
(κ)	0.56	0.84	0.93	0.94	0.92	**0.96**

Table 2.5 shows the average accuracies obtained by SRC, JSRC, MSSRC, MASRC, DSDL and the proposed CASRC techniques. From this table, one can see that the proposed technique provides results similar to those obtained by the best literature method (i.e., the MASRC technique). For qualitative analysis, Figure 2-7 displays the classification maps generated by the different techniques.

In the second experiment, the standard training and test set of the Indian Pines dataset is used for comparison. Table 2.5 also reports the classification results obtained by the different techniques using the standard training and test set. From the table, one can see that, as in the case of the University of Pavia dataset, the proposed technique also provides better results for this dataset. The proposed technique has an OA of 96.29%, and an AA of 97.55% which are at least 2% more than the best result provided by the existing methods. This again shows the effectiveness of the proposed technique in modelling better spatial information.

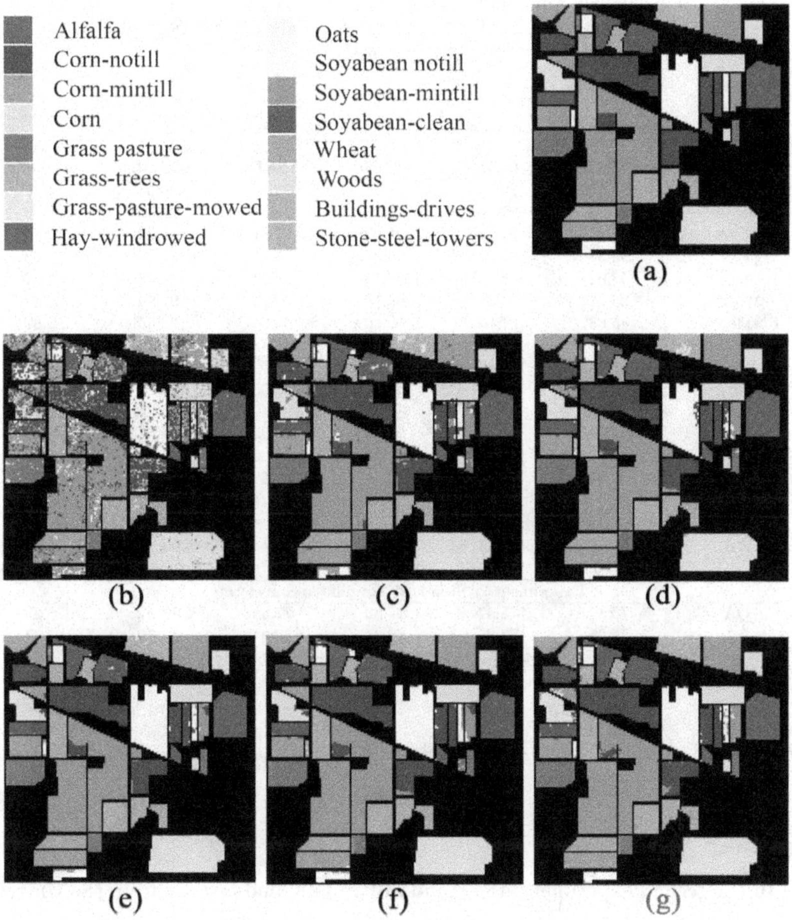

Figure 2-7: Indian Pines dataset a) Ground truth image. Classification maps generated by b) SRC, c) JSRC, d) MSSRC, e) MASRC, f) DSDL and g) proposed CASRC.

University of Houston 2013

Like the Indian Pines dataset, for this dataset 10% of labelled samples from each class are randomly selected for training and the rest 90% are used for testing. Table 2.6 reports the average OA, AA and κ obtained by the different techniques for five runs. From the table, one can see that our CASRC technique with $\overline{OA}$ of

Table 2.6: Classification results obtained by the SRC [28], JSRC [29], MSSRC [268], MASRC[56], DSDL[224] and proposed CASRC (University of Houston 2013 dataset).

Experiment 1: Randomly Chosen Training and Test Sets (five runs)						
Class Name	**SRC**	**JSRC**	**MSSRC**	**MASRC**	**DSDL**	**Proposed CASRC**
Grass Healthy	97.58	99.47	99.57	99.63	99.64	91.71
Grass Stresses	98.24	97.20	98.90	98.28	99.56	96.03
Grass Synthetic	99.68	97.86	98.92	99.81	100.00	96.84
Tree	95.51	99.84	98.34	99.95	99.77	92.68
Soil	97.92	100.00	100.00	100.00	100.00	96.37
Water	96.71	94.25	99.18	95.41	97.53	99.42
Residential	85.68	87.82	89.90	90.36	92.55	92.80
Commercial	91.89	97.82	100.00	100.00	100.00	99.95
Road	81.74	96.55	98.01	94.99	98.54	94.44
Highway	90.25	98.17	98.82	98.55	99.20	97.01
Railway	78.60	96.17	100.00	94.42	100.00	99.11
Parking Lot 1	84.65	98.81	99.46	98.97	99.62	98.43
Parking Lot 2	35.07	74.17	87.96	56.02	84.55	99.46
Tennis Court	98.08	96.42	100.00	99.69	100.00	99.60
Running Track	98.65	99.80	95.29	100.00	100.00	98.50
$\overline{OA}$	89.66 $\pm$0.47	96.51 $\pm$0.75	97.83 $\pm$0.47	96.17 $\pm$0.86	**98.37** $\pm$0.58	97.60 $\pm$0.51
$\overline{AA}$	88.68$\pm$0.52	95.62 $\pm$0.63	97.55 $\pm$0.61	94.86 $\pm$0.95	**97.93** $\pm$0.69	97.45 $\pm$0.58
$\overline{\kappa}$	0.89$\pm$0.00	0.96 $\pm$0.00	0.98$\pm$0.00	0.96$\pm$0.00	**0.98**$\pm$0.00	0.97$\pm$0.00
Experiment 2: Standard Training and Test Sets						
OA	73.37	75.47	77.82	77.58	**80.32**	78.29
AA	77.25	77.35	80.32	80.04	**82.79**	81.07
κ	0.71	0.74	0.76	0.76	**0.79**	0.77

97.60% and $\overline{AA}$ of 97.45% is comparable with the best result produced by DSDL technique. Figure 2-8 displays the classification maps generated by the different techniques.

In the second experiment, the standard training and test set from the University of Houston 2013 dataset were used for comparison. Table 2.6 also reports the classification results of the different techniques. The results presented in this table demonstrate that the proposed technique performs better than most state-of-the-art techniques and similarly to DSDL in this experiment. Note that the DSDL technique uses multiscale superpixels for defining adaptive windows. Thus, the inclusion of spatial information is dependent on the size and number of adaptive windows used, which is varied from image to image. Whereas, the proposed technique defines adaptive multiscale windows by using connected components of the image. It is capable of incorporating appropriate spatial information for a variety of images.

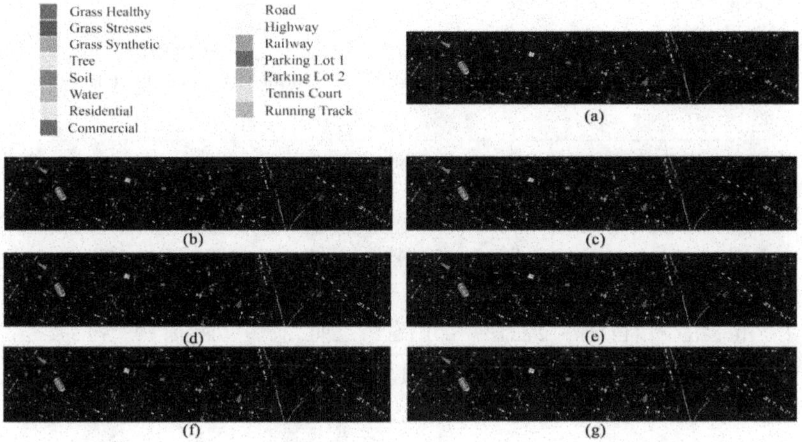

Figure 2-8: University of Houston 2013 dataset: a) Ground truth image. Classification maps generated by b) SRC, c) JSRC, d) MSSRC, e) MASRC, f) DSDL and g) proposed CASRC

Computation Time

To demonstrate the computational efficiency of the proposed technique, we compare its execution time with that of existing techniques. Table 2.7 presents the computational time in seconds (s) required by the different techniques for both randomly selected and standard training and test set configurations. From the table, one can see that both the SRC and the JSRC techniques are consuming significantly less time compared to the other techniques. Since, the SRC does not include spatial information in classification, it provides the results in least time. On the other hand, the JSRC uses only a single window to incorporate spatial information. In order to incorporate better spatial information, the MSSRC, MASRC and DSDL used multiscale windows, and from the experiments it is found that the classification results provided by the DSDL and MASRC are better than those of the MSSRC. The proposed CASRC technique, which is also a multiscale approach, takes generally lesser time than the best state-of-the-art techniques. This is because the CASRC technique exploited connected components to define spatial windows which include comparatively less number of neighbour pixels by avoiding irrelevant pixels.

Table 2.7: Computational time in seconds (s) taken by SRC, JSRC, MSSRC, MASRC, DSDL and the proposed CASRC techniques for different datasets.

Experiment 1: Randomly Chosen Training and Test Sets						
Dataset	**SRC**	**JSRC**	**MSSRC**	**MASRC**	**DSDL**	**Proposed CASRC**
Pavia	18.78s	66.88s	149.94s	1883.40s	1301.73s	1096.36s
Indian Pines	4.59s	15.15s	10.38s	271.17s	138.31s	100.09s
Houston	12.00s	25.39s	691.14s	236.73s	498.59s	479.59s
Experiment 2: Standard Training and Test Sets						
Pavia	26.00s	88.05s	196.32s	2432.93s	1930.88	1440.97s
Indian Pines	3.79s	15.91s	9.14s	203.35s	113.18s	82.21s
Houston	12.26s	30.87s	776.54s	299.62s	600.08s	511.67s

2.3.3 Discussion

By analysing the classification results obtained in the experiments one can see that the SRC technique, that does not take into account spatial information, provides worst results for all the three considered datasets. The JSRC technique that uses only a single window to define the spatial neighbourhood failed to provide better results than the multiscale windows based techniques. The multiscale techniques MSSRC, MASRC and DSDL are all providing improved results, but they have some limitations. The MSSRC uses a segmentation algorithm to define the multiscale windows. It performs well on the University of Pavia and the University of Houston 2013 datasets, where segmentation results provided good spatial information. It produces poor result for the Indian Pines dataset, where segmentation results failed to provide good spatial information. The MASRC and DSDL uses multiscale square windows and multiscale adaptive windows, respectively, of increasing size to incorporate spatial information. Since, optimum spatial information is dependent on the number and size of these windows and also varied from image to image, the results of both these techniques relied on these windows. Thus, considering the same parameters setting, the MASRC and DSDL failed to provide consistent results for all the datasets. Furthermore, the performance of DSDL method also relies on how well the dictionary is trained for all the classes. As demonstrated in the Indian Pines dataset, classes with few training samples failed to train the dictionary properly, hence reducing the model's overall performance. On the other hand, the proposed CASRC provides consistent and good results for all the datasets. This is because the CASRC technique defines the multiscale windows by exploiting the connected components of the image. Since these windows are adaptive to the shape of the objects in the image, the spatial neighbourhoods defined by these windows provided better spatial information. Furthermore, we have shown that the modified max-tree (min-tree) in our proposed technique successfully mitigates the limitations of the existing max-tree (min-tree) for defining better spatial neighborhoods.

2.4 Conclusion

The inclusion of spatial information in sparse classifiers has significantly improved their performance. To incorporate contextual information for classification of unlabelled pixels, the spatial neighbourhoods (either fixed or variable shape windows) defined by the literature methods have some limitations. In this chapter, we exploited connected components of the image for defining better spatial neighbourhood of each unlabelled pixel. To this end, we proposed a novel technique that construct modified max-tree and modified min-tree to represent different connected components of the image based on the predefined thresholds. The filter images obtained from both the modified max-tree and the modified min-tree by considering multiple thresholds are then used as reference images. Finally, the shapes of the windows that represent spatial neighbourhoods of each unlabelled pixel are defined by looking into the surrounding connected components present in the reference images. Since the windows corresponding to an unlabelled pixel are determined by looking into the connected components surrounding it, the size and shape of these windows are adaptive in nature and retains only the neighbour pixels belonging to the homogeneous region.

The effectiveness of the proposed technique has been assessed through comparisons with five state-of-the-art methods using three distinct HSI datasets. The experimental results consistently demonstrate that, unlike the state-of-the-art methods, the proposed technique yields good performance across all considered datasets. For more challenging standard training and test sets provided by the remote sensing community, the proposed technique exhibited significantly enhanced accuracy, with improvements that exceeded 5% compared to the best method in the literature. In this research, the proposed technique exploited *area* attribute to define component adaptive spatial windows. Exploitation of other attributes will be an interesting future development of this work. Furthermore, the filter images generated by the proposed technique depend on user-defined thresholds. Although this is not a critical parameter, for further improvement we plan to use optimization techniques such as swarm optimization to find the optimal thresholds.

Chapter 3

Dictionary Learning using Novel Multiscale Context Sensitive Spectral Features for Classification of Hyperspectral Imagery

3.1 Introduction

Improving the quality of the dictionary will definitely increase the performance of SRC. A simple way of achieving this is by increasing the number of labelled samples (atoms) for each class. But in doing so, the size of the dictionary will increase, leading to an increase in the labelling cost and computational burden. Thus, the focus shifts to another approach of building a quality dictionary called *dictionary learning*. In dictionary learning, the effectiveness of a classifier is dependent on the discriminative power of the patterns (pixels) used to learn the dictionary. In this thesis, to learn compact, qualitative, and comprehensive dictionaries, each pixel is represented by a feature set extracted by considering its relevant spatial neighborhood. Note that in contrast to the first approach, a simple and computationally efficient technique is proposed to define each pixel's appropriate spatial neighbourhoods. Then, instead of using the spatial contextual information from it directly, a feature extraction method was proposed that exploits this information to extract the discriminative features of each pixel.

In the literature, several dictionary learning methods have been proposed that aims to build discriminative and comprehensive dictionaries. In [1], Aharon *et al.* proposed the K-singular value decomposition (K-SVD) dictionary learning algorithm by minimizing the representation error of the dictionary. To improve discrimination power of the dictionary, Zhang *et al.* proposed an extended version of K-SVD algorithm called Discriminative K-SVD (DKSVD) [267]. Along with the representation error, DKSVD also minimizes the classification error. To further refine this, Jiang *et al.* proposed the Label Consistent K-SVD (LCKSVD) algorithm by including the sparse code error into the optimization function [103]. Besides using K-SVD, Liu et al. developed a class-guided coupled dictionary learning to handle multispectral and hyperpsectral information fusion for collaborative classification [137]. Other methods such as FDDL [252], LSDDL [75], class-wise DL [82] and S-DLR [67] were also proposed to produce discriminative dictionaries by embedding interclass and intraclass information into the objective function.

Due to the inherent noise in HSIs, the effectiveness of the aforementioned techniques is limited, since only spectral features are used to construct the dictionary. In the literature, it is already established that the incorporation of contextual information greatly improves the representative and discriminative power of a pixel [17, 90, 254]. As a results several techniques incorporate contextual information of the pixels to learn a better dictionary. The contextual information is added either before the dictionary learning process [131, 240, 247] or during the classification process [57, 224]. In [240], Wang *et al.* propose a semi-supervised dictionary learning model that uses a fixed-size window to increase the number of training samples followed by learning a dictionary through a joint sparsity model. Lin *et al.* propose a similar dictionary learning model, but uses superpixels instead of a fixed-size window to increase the training samples [131]. In [247], Xue *et al.* use a tensor low rank sparse representation model to maintain contextual and global information followed by an incremental dictionary learning scheme to build a dictionary for classification. Alternatively, Fang *et al.* introduce an algorithm called class-labelled orthogonal matching pursuit to learn the dictionary and then use it to approximate a group of pixels within a superpixel [57]. In [224], a discriminant sub-dictionary learning method was proposed for dictionary construction. This approach incorporates a global discriminative constraint term into the energy function of the K-SVD algorithm. The resulting learned dictionary was subsequently utilized within an adaptive multiscale sparse representation framework for HSI classification. In addition to contextual information, several approaches utilize spatial features for the construction of dictionary. Ma *et al.* extracted multiple spatial features and combined them with spectral features to learn the dictionary [145]. Song *et al.* used eigen features to learn the dictionary [201]. Hajiani *et al.* used dictionary learning to extract better features for HSI classification [78].

In dictionary learning, the incorporation of contextual information or spatial features has shown promising results. Contextual information offers the advantage of minimizing the uncertainty of spectral features, but it may decrease the sensitivity to the fine details necessary for class discrimination. Whereas, spatial features offer detailed characteristics of objects, but the extraction process can lead to the loss of useful information required for classification. Thus, in both cases, the consideration of appropriate spatial neighborhoods of the pixel is very important. In the present work, a novel method was proposed, called discriminative K-singular value decomposition using multiscale context-sensitive spectral features (DKSVD-MCSSF), which extracts robust features by exploiting singular value decomposition (SVD) to build dictionaries for the classification of HSI. Our method first uses superpixels and a fixed window to identify the appropriate spatial neighborhoods of the pixel. Then, considering the spatial neighborhoods of the pixel, SVD is used to extract the context-sensitive spectral features of it. The extracted features are finally used to learn the dictionaries for the HSI classification. The main contributions of this research work are: (i) It proposes a technique to identify appropriate spatial neighborhoods of pixels on the input image; (ii) It exploits SVD to extract novel context-sensitive spectral features for dictionary learning; and (iii) It offers higher computational efficiency compared to many state-of-the-art techniques. The experiments were conducted on three real hyperspectral datasets. The results show the effectiveness of the proposed technique.

The organization of this chapter is as follows. Section 3.3 presents the proposed method in detail. Experimental results and analysis are reported in Section 3.4. Finally, Section 3.5 gives the concluding remarks.

3.2 Background

Our proposed technique exploits both Singular Value Decomposition (SVD) and a Discriminative K-SVD dictionary learning technique. A brief description of these methods is provided in the subsequent subsections.

Given HSI $\mathbf{H} \in \mathbb{R}^{P \times Q \times B}$, with $P \times Q$ denoting the spatial size of the image and B the number of bands, the strategy of a sparse representation classifier involves finding a linear combination of atoms for an unknown pixel $y \in \mathbb{R}^{B}$ such that:

3.2.1 Singular Value Decomposition (SVD)

Similar to eigen decomposition, SVD is a decomposition technique used to extract the characteristics of a matrix [109]. However, unlike eigen decomposition which can be applied only to square matrices, SVD can be used to decompose rectangular matrices as well. The SVD of a rectangular matrix E of size $m \times n$ is given as:

$$\mathrm{E} = \mathrm{U}\Sigma\mathrm{V}^{\mathrm{T}}$$

where, U is a $m \times m$ matrix, Σ is a $m \times n$ diagonal matrix and V is a $n \times n$ matrix. The matrix U is called the left singular matrix, and it consists of orthogonal column vectors such that the first column vector holds the maximum possible information of the column space of E, the second vector holds the maximum remaining information of the column space and so on. The matrix V is called the right singular matrix, and it consists of orthogonal column vectors that represent the information across the row space of E. Σ is a diagonal matrix, and its diagonal entries contain singular values in decreasing order.

3.2.2 Discriminative K-SVD (DKSVD)

DKSVD is an extended version of K-SVD dictionary learning algorithm. In order to further improve the dictionary, DKSVD incorporates an additional classification error into the optimization function of K-SVD in Equation 1.21 to learn a dictionary and a linear classifier that is both representative and discriminative [267]. The term $||\mathrm{G} - \mathrm{W}\mathrm{A}_{\mathrm{G}}||_F^2$ computes classification error, where $\mathrm{G} = [g_1, g_2, \ldots, g_M] \in \mathbb{R}^{C\times M}$ is the class matrix of training samples, $g_i = [0, \ldots, 1, \ldots, 0]^T \in \mathbb{R}^C$ is a class vector and $\mathrm{W} \in \mathbb{R}^{C\times N}$ is a linear classifier.Thus, the objective function of DKSVD is formulated as follows:

$$\{\hat{\mathrm{D}}, \hat{\mathrm{A}}_{\mathrm{Z}}, \hat{\mathrm{W}}\} = \underset{\mathrm{D},\mathrm{A}_{\mathrm{Z}},\mathrm{W}}{\arg\min} ||\mathrm{Z} - \mathrm{D}\mathrm{A}_{\mathrm{Z}}||_{\mathrm{F}}^2 + \gamma||\mathrm{G} - \mathrm{W}\mathrm{A}_{\mathrm{Z}}||_F^2 \tag{3.1}$$

$$s.t \;\; ||\alpha_j||_0 < K, j = 1, 2, \ldots, M$$

Equation (3.1) can also be written as:

$$\{\hat{\mathrm{D}}, \hat{\mathrm{A}}_{\mathrm{Z}}, \hat{\mathrm{W}}\} = \underset{\mathrm{D},\mathrm{A}_{\mathrm{Z}},\mathrm{W}}{\arg\min} \left\| \begin{pmatrix} \mathrm{Z} \\ \sqrt{\gamma}\mathrm{G} \end{pmatrix} - \begin{pmatrix} \mathrm{D} \\ \sqrt{\gamma}\mathrm{W} \end{pmatrix} \mathrm{A}_{\mathrm{Z}} \right\|_F^2 \tag{3.2}$$

$$s.t \;\; ||\alpha_j||_0 < K, j = 1, 2, \ldots, M$$

where γ is a regularization parameter that tunes the contribution of the classification error. This is an empirical scalar whose value can be adjusted based on the specific application. By using the notations, $\mathrm{Z}^* = \begin{pmatrix} \mathrm{Z} \\ \sqrt{\gamma}\mathrm{G} \end{pmatrix}$ and $\mathrm{D}^* = \begin{pmatrix} \mathrm{D} \\ \sqrt{\gamma}\mathrm{W} \end{pmatrix}$,

Equation (3.2) can be rewritten as:

$$\{\hat{D^*}, \hat{A}_Z\} = \underset{D^*, A_Z}{\arg\min} \|Z^* - D^* A_Z\|_F^2 \quad s.t \, \|\alpha_j\|_0 < K, j = 1, 2, \ldots, M \tag{3.3}$$

which can easily be solved using K-SVD algorithm.

3.3 Proposed Technique

Dictionaries learnt by adding contextual information or by using spatial features have already shown their effectiveness in pattern classification. In this work, we extract novel multiscale context-sensitive spectral features to be used for dictionary learning. The entire framework of our proposed technique is depicted in Figure 3-1, and it consists of the following five sequential steps: 1) Identification of the appropriate neighbourhood of the pixels, 2) Extraction of context-sensitive spectral features (CSSF) of pixels, 3) Generation of multiscale CSSF, 4) Learning dictionaries using DKSVD, and 5) Classification of the HSI. The details of each of these steps are given in the following subsections.

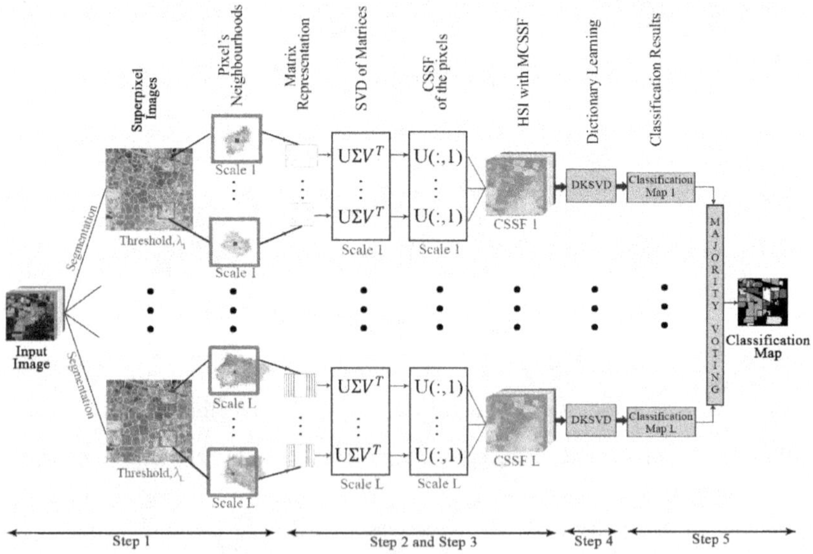

Figure 3-1: Illustration of the framework of the proposed method.

3.3.1 Identification of the appropriate neighbourhood of the pixels

In order to use incorporate spatial contextual information in dictionary learning, identifying the appropriate pixel neighborhood is important. The use of a fixed window is an overly simple approach to model this contextual information and has significant limitations, especially when border pixels are involved. To mitigate this problem, a superpixel-based approach was used. In this approach, a superpixel image is generated from the input image. Then the pixel itself and its surrounding pixels within the same superpixel are considered as the neighbourhood. Since superpixel algorithms merge homogeneous regions of the input image on the basis of a given threshold value, the size of the superpixel depends on the threshold being used. In some cases, they are formed by merging multiple regions that are associated to different objects, resulting in an under-segmentation of the image. As a result, this approach may not incorporate appropriate contextual information. To mitigate the drawbacks of the above approaches, in this work we exploit both the fixed-size window and superpixel to identify better neighbour pixels where each one avoids the drawback of the other.

In greater detail, let S denote the superpixel image derived from the input HSI $\mathbf{H}$ by applying a superpixel algorithm with threshold value λ. For a pixel y and a fixed window J centered at y, J_y represents the set of pixels inside the window J in $\mathbf{H}$ and S_y represents the set of pixels in $\mathbf{H}$ associated with the superpixel of y. In our work, the appropriate neighbourhood of pixel y is identified as $J_y \cap S_y$, that is, it contains both pixels that belong to the superpixel and those inside the window. This concept is visually illustrated in Figure 3-1 where the fixed-size window is represented by the red square, while the area within the cyan boundary represents the superpixel. The gray portion (i.e. the intersection of fixed-size window and superpixel) is considered as the spatial neighbourhood of the pixel.

3.3.2 Extraction of context-sensitive spectral features (CSSF)

Once the spatial neighbourhood of the pixels is identified, the proposed technique proceeds to extract spectral features considering the spectral information of these neighboring pixels. Since the spectral features of the pixels are extracted by incorporating their neighbour pixels, we call it the context-sensitive spectral feature (CSSF). Our proposed technique exploits SVD to extract CSSF from pixels as follows.

Let y be a pixel in the input image $\mathbf{H}$. The pixel y and its neighbouring pixels, identified by applying the method presented in Subsection 3.3.1 are stored in a matrix $\mathrm{E_y} \in \mathbb{R}^{B\times R}$, where B denotes the number of spectral bands and R represents the number of pixels in the defined neighborhood of y. Now, SVD is applied to decompose the matrix $\mathrm{E_y}$ into $\mathrm{U_y}, \Sigma_\mathrm{y}$, and $\mathrm{V_y}$ such that $\mathrm{E_y} = \mathrm{U_y}\Sigma_\mathrm{y}\mathrm{V_y^T}$. The column space of $\mathrm{E_y}$ is spanned by the spectral values of the neighboring pixels of y, and the first column of the left singular vector matrix $\mathrm{U_y}$ contains the maximum possible information within this column space. Thus, the first column of $\mathrm{U_y} \in \mathbb{R}^{B\times 1}$ provides context-sensitive spectral information of pixel y. In this investigation, the components of the first column of $\mathrm{U_y}$ are considered CSSF of the pixel y.

3.3.3 Generation of multiscale CSSF

As mentioned above, the extraction of CSSF for every pixel in the input image is performed by considering its spatial neighbourhood. The spatial neighbourhood of a pixel is determined from a superpixel generated by using a threshold λ. As it is very difficult to generate an optimal superpixel image considering a single threshold, the spatial neighbourhood of the pixels identified from a single superpixel image may not provide sufficient contextual information of the pixels. To incorporate better contextual information, we generate multiple superpixel images by varying the threshold value. Then, for each superpixel image, the appropriate neighbourhood of the pixels is identified by using the method presented in Subsection 3.3.1 and the corresponding CSSF of the pixels are extracted by the method presented in Subsection 3.3.2. Thus, for a pixel on the input image, a multiple set of context-sensitive spectral features called multiscale CSSF (MCSSF) are extracted by considering its neighbour information at different scales. The extracted set of CSSF (i.e., MCSSF) incorporates detailed spatial information of the pixel in the input image. Once MCSSF are extracted, for each CSSF a dictionary is learned by adopting DKSVD dictionary learning algorithm.

Algorithm 3 Proposed DKSVD-MCSSF

Input: Hyperspectral Image $\mathbf{H}$; sparsity level K; set of threshold values ($\lambda_1 < \lambda_2 < \cdots < \lambda_L$), Total number of pixels $T = P \times Q$

// **Segment the input image to extract superpixel**
for i=1 to L **do**
  $S_i = segment_{\lambda_i}(\mathbf{H})$
end for

// **Extract MCSSF**
for i=1 to L **do**
  for j=1 to T **do**
    $\mathrm{E}_\mathrm{i}^\mathrm{j} = vectorized(\mathrm{J}_\mathrm{i}^\mathrm{j} \cap \mathrm{S}_\mathrm{i}^\mathrm{j})$
    $SVD(\mathrm{E}_\mathrm{i}^\mathrm{j}) = \mathrm{U}\Sigma\mathrm{V}^\mathrm{T}$
    $x_i^j = U(:, 1)$
  end for
  i^{th} CSSF $= [x_i^1, x_i^2, \ldots, x_i^T] \in \mathbb{R}^{P \times Q \times B}$
end for

// **Dictionary Learning using DKSVD-MCSSF**
for i=1 to L **do**
  Solve Equation (3.4), Equation (3.5) and Equation (3.6) to obtain $\hat{\mathrm{D}}_{\mathrm{Z_i}}$ and $\hat{\mathrm{W}}_{\mathrm{Z_i}}$
end for
for each unlabelled pixel x **do**
  for i=1 to L **do**
    Solve Equation (3.7) obtain sparse coefficient $\hat{A}_{X_i}$
    Compute c_i^x using Equation Equation (3.8) and Equation (3.9)
  end for
  assign class label to x using the majority voting scheme.
end for

3.3.4 Learning dictionaries using DKSVD

Let the proposed technique considers $\lambda_1, \lambda_2, \ldots, \lambda_L$ thresholds for extracting L CSSF sets to represent each pixel of the image. The matrix $\mathrm{Z_i}$ contains the training pixels represented with the ith CSSF set, such that $\mathrm{Z_i} = [\mathrm{Z_i^1}, \mathrm{Z_i^2}, \ldots, \mathrm{Z_i^C}] \in \mathbb{R}^{B\times M}$, where $\mathrm{Z_i^j}$ is the subset of training samples taken from class j. The matrix $\mathrm{D_{Z_i}}$ represents the dictionary learnt by using $\mathrm{Z_i}$, such that $\mathrm{D_{Z_i}} = [\mathrm{D_i^1}, \mathrm{D_i^2}, \ldots, \mathrm{D_i^C}] \in \mathbb{R}^{B\times N}$. The optimization function of DKSVD presented in Equation (3.3) can be defined as:

$$\{\hat{\mathrm{D}}^*_{\mathrm{Z_i}}, \hat{\mathrm{A}}_{\mathrm{Z_i}}\} = \underset{\mathrm{D}^*_{\mathrm{Z_i}}, \mathrm{A}_{\mathrm{Z_i}}}{\arg\min} \; \|\mathrm{Z_i^*} - \mathrm{D}^*_{\mathrm{Z_i}}\mathrm{A}_{\mathrm{Z_i}}\|_F^2 \tag{3.4}$$

$$s.t \; \|\alpha_{j_i}\|_0 < K, j = 1, 2, \ldots, M \; and \; i = 1, 2, \ldots, L$$

In Equation (3.4), the dictionary $\mathrm{D_{Z_i}}$ and the classifier $\mathrm{W_{Z_i}}$ associated to the training set $\mathrm{Z_i}$ and class matrix $\mathrm{G_i}$ are jointly optimized and their combined normalized values are stored in $\mathrm{D}^*_{\mathrm{Z_i}}$. For the training set $\mathrm{Z_i}$ ($i = 1, 2, \ldots, L$), the corresponding dictionary $\hat{\mathrm{D}}_{\mathrm{Z_i}}$ and the classifier $\hat{\mathrm{W}}_{\mathrm{Z_i}}$ are obtained by using Equation3.5 and Equation3.6.

$$\hat{\mathrm{D}}_{\mathrm{Z_i}} = \left\{ \frac{d_i^1}{\|d_i^1\|_2}, \frac{d_i^2}{\|d_i^2\|_2}, \ldots, \frac{d_i^N}{\|d_i^N\|_2} \right\} \tag{3.5}$$

$$\hat{\mathrm{W}}_{\mathrm{Z_i}} = \left\{ \frac{w_i^1}{\|d_i^1\|_2}, \frac{w_i^2}{\|d_i^2\|_2}, \ldots, \frac{w_i^N}{\|d_i^N\|_2} \right\} \tag{3.6}$$

Since our proposed method uses MCSSF to learn the dictionaries by adopting the DKSVD dictionary learning technique, we named it DKSVD-MCSSF.

3.3.5 Classification of HSI

After the dictionaries and classifiers are trained with L multiscale CSSF, the last step is to classify the pixels of the HSI. To classify an unknown pixel x, first, the CSSF of the pixel x and its neighbouring pixels are stored in a matrix.Let the matrix $\mathrm{X_i} = \{x_1^{CSSF_i}, x_2^{CSSF_i}, \ldots, x_R^{CSSF_i}\}$ represents R neighbouring pixels of x with their i^{th} CSSF set. Then, following the steps of the JSRC, the sparse coefficient $\mathrm{A_{X_i}}(i = 1, 2, \ldots, L)$ associated with the matrix $\mathrm{X_i}$ can be obtained as follows:

$$\hat{\mathrm{A}}_{\mathrm{X_i}} = \arg\min \|\mathrm{X_i} - \hat{\mathrm{D}}_{\mathrm{Z_i}} \mathrm{A_{X_i}}\| \tag{3.7}$$

$$s.t \; \|\mathrm{A_{X_i}}\|_{row,0} < K \; and \, i = 1, 2, \ldots, L$$

Once the sparse coefficient $\mathrm{A_{X_i}}$ is obtained, with the help of the linear classifier $\hat{\mathrm{W}}_{\mathrm{Z_i}}$ we calculate the class label matrix $\mathrm{H_i}$:

$$\mathrm{G_i} = \hat{\mathrm{W}}_{\mathrm{Z_i}} \hat{\mathrm{A}}_{\mathrm{X_i}} \tag{3.8}$$

where, $\mathrm{G_i} = \{g_1, g_2, \ldots, g_R\} \in \mathbb{R}^{C \times R}$ and the vector g_r denotes the class information of the rth neighbour pixel. Then the class vector $\nu_i \in \mathbb{R}^{C \times 1}$ is obtained by summing up the elements in each row of G_i. Finally, the class label c_i^x of the pixel x represented with i^{th} CSSF is computed as:

$$c_i^{\mathbf{x}} = \arg\max\{\nu_i\} \quad for \quad i = 1, 2, \ldots, L \tag{3.9}$$

After predicting the class label of each $x_i, i = 1, 2, \ldots, L$, the proposed technique uses a majority voting scheme to assign the final class label to the unknown pixel x. The proposed method is called DKSVD-MCSSF as it generates MCSSF to learn the dictionaries by adopting DKSVD dictionary learning technique. Algorithm 3 summarizes the different steps of the proposed method.

3.4 Experimental Results

The details of the experimental setup and the results obtained by the different techniques are presented below.

3.4.1 Experimental Setup

In order to assess the proposed technique's effectiveness, three popular hyperspectral datasets i.e., University of Pavia, Indian Pines and University of Houston 2013 are used for its evaluation. The description of each of these datasets is given in Appendix A. We compared the proposed DKSVD-MCSSF technique with six state-of-the-art techniques such as label consistent K-SVD (LCKSVD) [103], joint sparse model-based DKSVD (JSM-DKSVD) [240], superpixel based discriminative sparse model (SBDSM) [57], discriminative sub-dictionary learning (DSDL) [224], superpixel wise low-rank approximation for partial label learning (SLAP) [254] and and Component Adaptive Sparse Representation Classification (CASRC) [17]. The LCKSVD technique does not consider contextual information to learn the dictionary. The JSM-DKSVD technique uses a single fixed-size window, whereas SBDSM, DSDL, and DKSVD-MCSSF exploits superpixel algorithms to incorporate contextual information in dictionary learning. SLAP and CASRC, while not a dictionary learning technique, are state-of-the-art spectral-spatial HSI classification techniques that consider spectral and spatial information of the pixel to classify HSI. The experiment was conducted over five independent runs, and the effectiveness of the various techniques was quantitatively assessed using three standard metrics: such as the average of overall accuracy ($\overline{OA}$), average accuracy ($\overline{AA}$) and Kappa accuracy ($\overline{\kappa}$).

To show the potentiality of the proposed technique irrespective of superpixel algorithms, experiments are conducted using SLIC [185, 206] and ISLIC [272]. To extract multiscale CSSFs of a pixel our proposed technique defines appropriate spatial neighbourhoods of the pixel by using a set of threshold values λ and a fixed window. In the present experiment for all the datasets $\lambda = [25, 50, 75, 100, 125, 150, 175, 200]$ and a fixed moderate size 17×17 window is considered. The number of iterations used to train the dictionary is fixed at 40. The value of the regularization parameter γ is varied within the range [1-5] without observing any significant variation in the classification results. Thus, it is fixed as 2 for all the datasets. Finally, the sparsity level K is always kept as 3.

Table 3.1: Training and testing samples for the University of Pavia, Indian Pines, and University of Houston 2013 datasets.

Indian Pines			Pavia University			University of Houston 2013		
Name	Training Sample	Testing Sample	Name	Training Sample	Testing Sample	Name	Training Sample	Testing Sample
Alfalfa	10	36	Asphalt	250	6381	Grass Healthy	126	1125
Corn-Notill	143	1285	Meadows	250	18399	Grass Stresses	126	1128
Corn-Mintill	83	747	Gravel	250	1849	Grass Synthetic	70	627
Corn	24	213	Broad Trees	250	2874	Tree	125	1119
Grass-Pasture	48	435	PMS	250	1095	Soil	125	1119
Grass-Trees	73	657	Bare Soil	250	4779	Water	33	292
Grs-Pas-Mow	10	18	Bitumen	300	1030	Residential	127	1141
Hay-Windrwd	48	430	SBB	250	3432	Commercial	125	1119
Oats	10	10	Shadows	250	697	Road	126	1126
Soyabean-Notill	97	875				Highway	123	1104
Soyabean-Mintill	246	2209				Railway	124	1111
Soyabean Clean	59	534				Parking Lot 1	124	1109
Wheat	21	184				Parking Lot 2	47	422
Woods	127	1138				Tennis Court	43	385
B-G-T-D	40	347				Running Track	66	594
Stone-Steel-Towers	10	83						

3.4.2 Results

In real case scenario, limited number of training samples are available. Therefore, in the experiment, we choose to select only a tiny portion of the total samples using a stratified sampling strategy for training and the rest are used for testing. Table 3.1 shows the different numbers of training and testing samples for each dataset.

3.4.2.1 Results: Indian Pines

For this dataset, only 10% of the total available labelled samples are randomly chosen as training samples and the rest 90% are used for testing. Table 3.2 shows the classification results of LCKSVD, SBDSM, JSM-DKSVD, DSDL,SLAP, CASRC and the proposed DKSVD-MCSSF technique using segmentation methods SLIC and ISLIC. From the table, one can see that the proposed technique performs better than the other state-of-the-art techniques. The $\overline{OA}$ of 98.88% and $\overline{AA}$ of 98.84% provided by the proposed technique are better than those provided by the best state-of-the-art method DSDL that results in an $\overline{OA}$ of 98.29% and an $\overline{AA}$ of 97.04%. Moreover, from the table it can be observed that the proposed technique

Table 3.2: Classification results obtained by the LCKSVD [103], SBDSM [57], JSM-DKSVD [240], DSDL[224], SLAP [254], CASRC [17] and DKSVD-MCSSF (Indian Pines dataset).

Class No.	LCKSVD (%)	SBDSM (%)		JSM-DKSVD (%)	DSDL (%)		SLAP (%)	CASRC (%)	Proposed DKSVD-MCSSF (%)	
	-	SLIC	ISLIC	-	SLIC	ISLIC	-	-	SLIC	ISLIC
1	57.78	100.00	97.22	92.78	97.22	93.89	100.00	96.10	100.00	98.61
2	54.38	86.99	90.57	92.79	97.59	95.24	90.04	96.47	98.79	97.86
3	50.79	83.67	92.80	93.25	98.98	94.94	94.11	96.47	98.82	99.30
4	33.80	99.06	89.77	91.08	95.68	88.45	88.54	91.27	99.41	99.18
5	82.99	86.34	93.01	96.51	96.60	95.40	96.59	93.84	94.77	97.47
6	91.54	96.19	99.09	97.20	99.79	99.70	98.84	99.82	99.85	100.00
7	64.44	100.00	96.67	95.56	93.33	97.78	95.20	92.00	100.00	100.00
8	95.21	100.00	98.84	99.67	100.00	99.81	98.42	99.95	100.00	99.88
9	58.00	92.00	100.00	90.00	90.00	100.00	91.11	94.44	100.00	100.00
10	58.79	87.36	80.00	94.26	95.27	94.70	93.07	95.68	96.60	98.00
11	71.32	87.71	90.84	96.03	99.16	98.56	98.73	98.71	99.29	99.29
12	44.08	81.84	80.11	90.56	96.44	91.65	92.98	96.44	97.84	97.85
13	85.54	99.46	98.70	96.09	99.46	99.24	99.46	99.46	100.00	98.91
14	89.82	97.59	98.91	98.54	99.79	99.63	99.53	99.68	100.00	100.00
15	39.19	97.92	89.94	90.64	99.25	96.47	99.95	98.50	99.71	99.49
16	88.43	90.12	98.07	92.77	94.22	96.63	90.12	94.05	100.00	98.80
$\overline{OA}$	68.19 ± 0.74	90.22 ± 0.93	91.58 ± 0.83	95.00 ± 0.37	98.29 ± 0.35	96.81 ± 0.50	95.88 ± 0.22	97.57 ± 0.42	98.83 ± 0.25	**98.94 ± 0.09**
$\overline{AA}$	66.63 ± 2.99	92.89 ± 0.97	93.33 ± 0.38	94.25 ± 0.53	97.04 ± 0.87	96.31 ± 0.61	95.23 ± 0.90	96.42 ± 0.84	**99.07 ± 0.21**	99.03 ± 0.11
$\overline{\kappa}$	0.64 ± 0.01	0.89 ± 0	0.90 ± 0.01	0.94 ± 0	0.98 ± 0	0.96 ± 0	0.95 ± 0	0.97 ± 0	**0.99 ± 0**	**0.99 ± 0**

is less sensitive to superpixel images generated by SLIC or ISLIC. Irrespective of SLIC or ISLIC, it always provides similar classification results. Whereas, the state-of-the-art methods SBDSM and DSDL are more sensitive to the superpixel image generated by different techniques. From Table 3.2, it can be seen that the classification performance of the DSDL method is increased from an $\overline{OA}$ of 96.81% and an $\overline{AA}$ of 96.31% to an $\overline{OA}$ of 98.29% and an $\overline{AA}$ of 97.04% by replacing ISLIC with SLIC. This shows the effectiveness of the proposed context-sensitive spectral feature for capturing better information of HSI. For a qualitative analysis, Figure 3-2 shows the classification maps provided by the different techniques. This figure illustrates that the methods that used multiscale approaches to capture spatial information provided smoother classification maps than the rest.

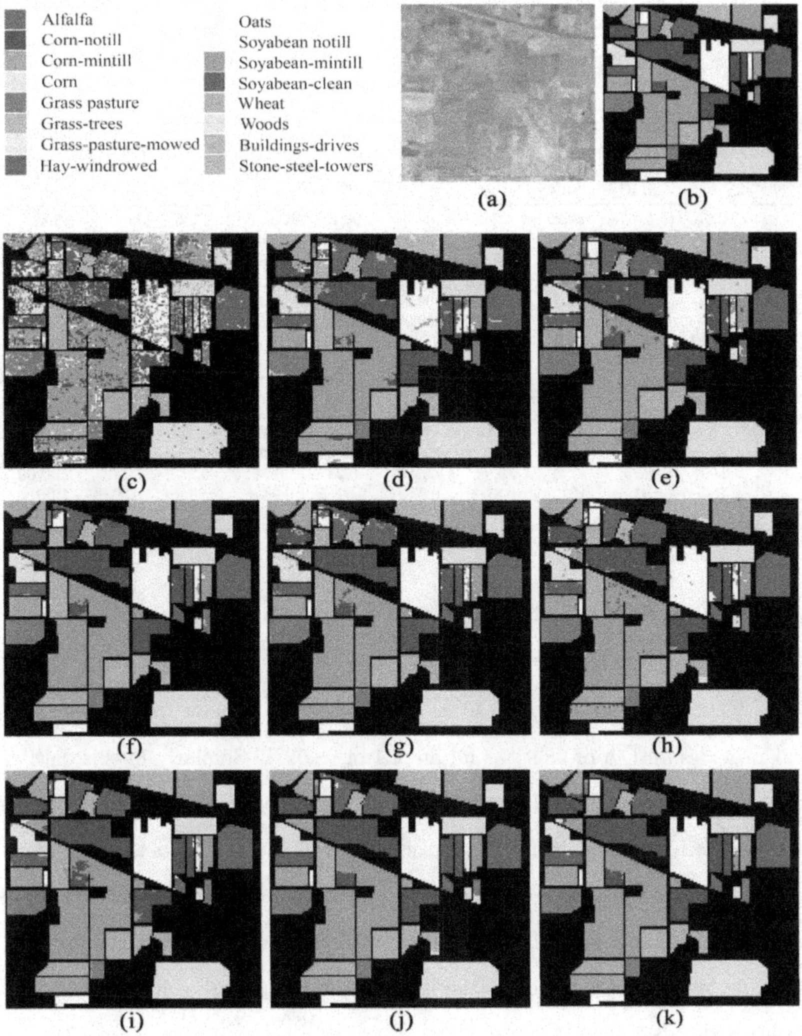

Figure 3-2: a) RGB Image b) Ground Truth of the Indian Pines dataset and the classification maps provided by c) LCKSVD d) SBDSM e) JSM-DKSVD f) DSDL(SLIC) g) DSDL(ISLIC) h)SLAP i) CASRC j) DKSVD-MCSSF(SLIC) and k) DKSVD-MCSSF(ISLIC)

3.4.2.2 Results: Pavia University

For this particular dataset, 250 samples from each class are chosen randomly as training samples and the rest are used for testing. Table 3.3 shows the classifica-

Table 3.3: Classification results obtained by the LCKSVD [103], SBDSM [57], JSM-DKSVD [240], DSDL[224], SLAP [254], CASRC [17] and DKSVD-MCSSF (University of Pavia dataset).

Class No.	**LCKSVD** (%)	**SBDSM** (%)		**JSM-DKSVD** (%)	**DSDL** (%)		**SLAP** (%)	**CASRC** (%)	**Proposed DKSVD-MCSSF** (%)	
	-	SLIC	ISLIC	-	SLIC	ISLIC	-	-	SLIC	ISLIC
1	63.62	79.67	82.26	72.29	94.34	93.15	98.51	97.46	98.14	99.24
2	79.87	96.01	95.34	93.55	99.59	99.06	98.09	99.24	99.71	99.87
3	70.24	98.10	97.05	95.93	99.85	99.49	98.69	100.00	99.73	99.91
4	91.93	90.24	95.25	96.23	96.32	95.47	94.37	95.45	97.46	97.98
5	99.71	98.52	98.54	99.96	99.54	99.80	99.43	99.96	99.68	100.00
6	70.85	97.73	92.46	88.12	99.99	99.67	99.59	99.86	99.99	99.8
7	87.50	99.67	98.93	99.57	100.00	99.65	99.56	99.93	99.96	100.00
8	73.28	94.60	96.38	92.63	99.41	98.44	98.46	99.41	99.49	99.58
9	98.48	75.70	97.33	98.22	67.75	95.90	99.74	96.21	99.08	99.16
$\overline{OA}$	77.14 ± 0.43	93.03 ± 0.95	93.31 ± 0.32	90.19 ± 0.44	98.04 ± 0.24	98.95 ± 0.22	98.23 ± 0.47	98.80 ± 0.22	99.31 ± 0.17	**99.62 ± 0.06**
$\overline{AA}$	81.72 ± 0.99	92.24 ± 0.65	94.84 ± 0.21	92.94 ± 0.38	95.19 ± 0.42	98.59 ± 0.23	98.49 ± 0.24	98.61 ± 0.27	99.21 ± 0.18	**99.51 ± 0.09**
$\overline{\kappa}$	0.70 ± 0.01	0.91 ± 0.01	0.91 ± 0	0.87 ± 0.01	0.97 ± 0	0.99 ± 0	0.98 ± 0	0.98 ± 0	0.99 ± 0	**1.00 ± 0**

tion results provided by different techniques. From the table, it can be seen that the proposed DKSVD-MCSSF technique provides the highest accuracy, with an $\overline{OA}$ of 99.03% and an $\overline{AA}$ of 99.16%. The best state-of-the-art method is DSDL that provides an $\overline{OA}$ of 98.95% and an $\overline{AA}$ of 98.59%. Similarly in this dataset, the change in the superpixel algorithm do not significantly affect the results of the proposed technique. This shows the robustness of the proposed CSSF in learning a better dictionary. The classification maps produced by different techniques are shown in Figure 3-3. It can be observed from this figure that the proposed technique incorporates better spatial information compared to the other state-of-the-art methods.

3.4.2.3 Results: University of Houston 2013

For University of Houston dataset, 10% of the total samples are chosen randomly as training samples and the rest are used for testing. The average OA, AA and Kappa obtained by different techniques are reported in Table 3.4. From the table, one can see that the proposed DKSVD-MCSSF provides better results as compared to the other state-of-the-art methods. In particular, it provides an $\overline{OA}$ of 99.21% and

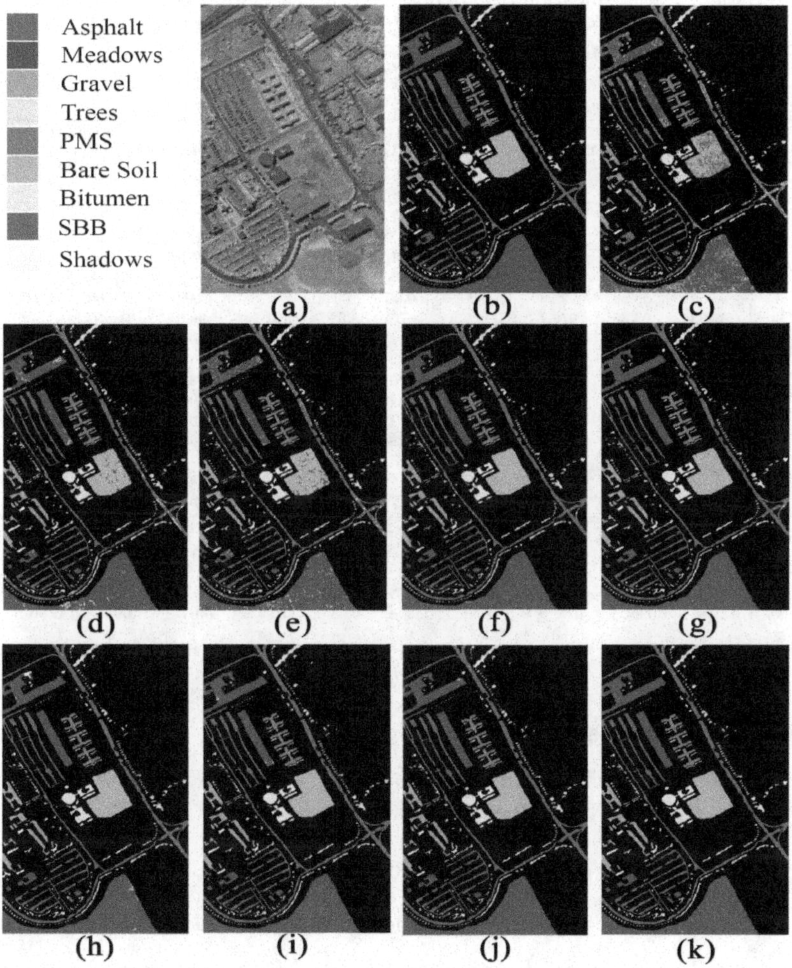

Figure 3-3: a) RGB Image b) Ground Truth of the Pavia University dataset and the classification maps provided by c) LCKSVD d) SBDSM e) JSM-DKSVD f) DSDL(SLIC) g) DSDL(ISLIC) h)SLAP i) CASRC j) DKSVD-MCSSF(SLIC) and k) DKSVD-MCSSF(ISLIC)

an $\overline{AA}$ of 98.99% for SLIC and an $\overline{OA}$ of 99.16% and an $\overline{AA}$ of 99.05% for ISLIC. This again shows the robustness of the proposed technique with respect to the segmentation methods used to generate the superpixel images. For a qualitative analysis, Figure 3-4 shows the classification maps obtained by different techniques. It can be observed that our proposed method provided smoother classification

Table 3.4: Classification results obtained by the LCKSVD [103], SBDSM [57], JSM-DKSVD [240], DSDL[224], SLAP [254], CASRC [17] and DKSVD-MCSSF (University of Houston 2013 dataset).

Class No.	LCKSVD (%)	SBDSM (%)		JSM-DKSVD (%)	DSDL (%)		SLAP (%)	CASRC (%)	Proposed DKSVD-MCSSF (%)	
	-	SLIC	ISLIC	-	SLIC	ISLIC	-	-	SLIC	ISLIC
1	96.84	99.09	97.87	99.20	99.57	99.34	95.61	99.64	99.91	99.73
2	99.01	98.49	95.69	99.24	99.54	99.36	97.22	95.57	99.73	99.76
3	99.74	97.22	77.54	99.39	99.11	100.00	99.52	98.98	99.64	99.76
4	96.48	98.80	97.64	99.91	99.27	99.95	96.78	99.62	99.69	99.91
5	98.50	99.82	99.28	100.00	100.00	100.00	97.58	100.00	100.00	100.00
6	96.23	94.66	97.67	99.25	94.73	96.85	94.24	96.64	98.37	97.86
7	86.05	88.27	89.29	91.92	88.94	93.78	90.06	89.48	98.55	97.68
8	91.74	97.57	97.32	95.98	96.93	96.18	80.00	96.73	98.31	95.58
9	83.57	95.15	95.35	95.91	97.90	97.32	86.31	98.40	99.84	99.93
10	88.66	98.19	97.59	98.93	100.00	99.62	95.52	99.75	99.82	99.86
11	79.30	96.98	98.54	97.53	100.00	99.39	92.31	99.42	99.08	98.78
12	84.13	98.81	97.57	99.24	98.88	97.40	89.64	99.19	99.08	98.78
13	36.26	72.80	76.78	82.42	93.74	82.46	49.24	87.16	93.36	97.57
14	97.97	100.00	99.22	97.25	100.00	100.00	98.12	100.00	100.00	98.51
15	99.16	99.39	99.46	99.93	100.00	99.93	97.54	99.53	99.79	100.00
$\overline{OA}$	89.90 ± 0.21	96.47 ± 0.33	95.27 ± 1.32	97.32 ± 0.38	98.06 ± 0.38	98.00 ± 0.49	94.54 ± 0.89	97.60 ± 0.29	**99.21 ± 0.13**	99.16 ± 0.21
$\overline{AA}$	88.90 ± 0.36	95.68 ± 0.62	94.42 ± 1.82	96.94 ± 0.39	97.90 ± 0.47	97.51 ± 0.57	94.37 ± 0.62	97.34 ± 0.38	98.99 ± 0.26	**99.05 ± 0.11**
$\overline{\kappa}$	0.89 ± 0	0.96 ± 0	0.95 ± 0.01	0.97 ± 0	0.98 ± 0	0.98 ± 0	0.94 ± 0	**0.97 ± 0**	**0.99 ± 0**	**0.99 ± 0**

maps than the compared ones.

3.4.3 Ablation Analysis

To incorporate spatial contextual information in the dictionary learning process, it is important to identify the appropriate neighbourhoods of the pixels in the image. To this end, our proposed technique extracts the MCSSF corresponding to each pixel of the input image with the help of both a fixed-size window and multiple superpixel images generated by different threshold values. Table 3.5 reports the performance of the proposed model by varying the fixed-size window from 5×5 to 25×25 pixels. From this table, one can see that across all the datasets, the proposed method provides the best results for 17×17 window. This aligns with the expectation that too small windows have insufficient contextual information, while excessively large windows increase the heterogeneity of the information, thereby limiting the extraction of informative features. Furthermore, to compare the ef-

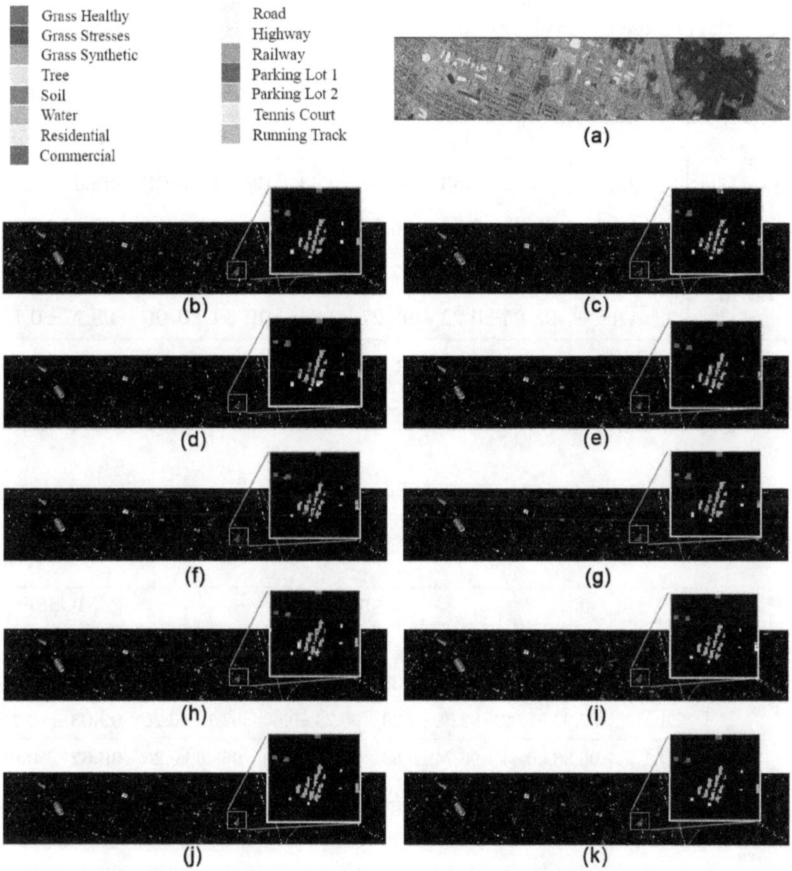

Figure 3-4: a) RGB Image b) Ground Truth of the University of Houston 2013 dataset and the classification maps provided by c) LCKSVD d) SBDSM e) JSM-DKSVD f) DSDL(SLIC) g) DSDL(ISLIC) h)SLAP i) CASRC j) DKSVD-MCSSF(SLIC) and k) DKSVD-MCSSF(ISLIC)

fectiveness of the proposed multiscale CSSF against siglescale CSSF, Table 3.6 reports the classification results provided by the CSSFs (extracted by considering different superpixel images) as well the MCSSF (extracted by considering multiple superpixel image). From the table, one can see that the proposed MCSSF exhibits significantly superior performance than all the individual CSSF extracted by considering different threshold values.

Table 3.5: Average of overall accuracy ($\overline{OA}$) and average accuracy ($\overline{AA}$) provided by the proposed DKSVD-MCSSF technique for windows of different sizes.

Dataset	Metric	Window size			
		(5 × 5)	(11 × 11)	(17 × 17)	(25 × 25)
Indian Pines	$\overline{OA}$	94.52±1.53	94.74±0.33	**98.94±0.09**	98.38±0.35
	$\overline{AA}$	92.45±2.14	96.34±0.23	**99.03±0.11**	98.48±0.29
Pavia	$\overline{OA}$	97.64±0.25	97.88±0.35	**99.62±0.06**	99.22±0.14
	$\overline{AA}$	98.25±0.22	98.27±0.24	**99.51±0.09**	98.77±0.15
Houston 2013	$\overline{OA}$	98.48±0.38	98.71±0.19	**99.16±0.21**	98.91±0.27
	$\overline{AA}$	98.30±0.35	98.75±0.28	**99.05±0.11**	98.84±0.31

Table 3.6: Average of overall accuracy ($\overline{OA}$) and average accuracy ($\overline{AA}$) provided by the proposed technique, considering different CSSFs extracted by varying the threshold λ and MCSSF.

Dataset	Metric	CSSF				MCSSF
		($\lambda = 25$)	($\lambda = 75$)	($\lambda = 125$)	($\lambda = 200$)	
Indian Pines	$\overline{OA}$	94.22±0.50	95.84±0.33	97.34±0.21	97.68±0.21	**98.94 ± 0.09**
	$\overline{AA}$	92.93±1.92	92.39±2.20	96.73±0.66	97.10±0.26	**99.03 ± 0.11**
Pavia	$\overline{OA}$	96.86±0.44	96.74±0.66	97.05±0.30	96.46±0.26	**99.62 ± 0.06**
	$\overline{AA}$	97.50±0.10	96.94±0.12	97.17±0.24	96.33±0.19	**99.51 ± 0.09**
Houston 2013	$\overline{OA}$	97.29±0.09	97.35±0.46	97.39±0.50	97.04±0.30	**99.16 ± 0.22**
	$\overline{AA}$	97.11±0.11	97.52±0.64	97.31±0.55	96.88±0.37	**99.05 ± 0.11**

Table 3.7: Computational time in seconds(s) taken by the LCKSVD, SBDSM, JSM-DKSVD, DSDL, SLAP, CASRC and DKSVD-MCSSF on the different datasets.

Dataset	LCKSVD	SBDSM	JSM-DKSVD	DSDL	SLAP	CASRC	Proposed DKSVD-MCSSF
Indian Pines	30.63s	33.17s	257.65s	129.16s	290.11s	123.70s	230.66s
Pavia	556.13s	583.89s	955.20s	1365.70s	1500.60s	1404.76s	608.77s
Houston	137.78s	234.20s	473.71s	610.24s	752.25s	585.88	322.35s

3.4.4 Computational Time

To demonstrate the computational efficiency of the proposed technique, the execution times in seconds taken by different techniques are reported in Table 3.7. For a fair comparison, the proposed technique and the four state-of-the-art methods were all implemented within the Matlab environment and executed on an identical personal computer. This system was configured with a 64-bit operating system, Intel(R) Core(TM) i5-10500 CPU clocked at 3.10GHz, and 24 GB of RAM.

From the table, one can see that the LCKSVD and the SBDSM take the least computing time as compared to the other methods. The LCKSVD provides the worst classification performance, as it considers only spectral information. The SBDSM provides better classification results than LCSVD, as it considers spatial information by generating a superpixel image. It uses DKSVD and class labelled OMP that take less time for dictionary learning as compared to the LCKSVD. The JSM-DKSVD increases the size of training samples by taking into account the neighbour samples. As a result, it takes a longer time to learn the dictionary, thus increasing the overall computing time. The DSDL yields the best accuracy among the state-of-the-art, but just like CASRC, it requires high computation time for large datasets. To incorporate better spatial information, both use multi-scale superpixel images in the classification stage, that increases their computing time. Among the six state-of-the-art methods considered in the experiment, SLAP resulted in the highest computation time for all datasets. On the other hand, the proposed technique uses multiscale context-sensitive features that contribute to decrease the computation time of both learning the dictionary and performing classification. The proposed method produces the best classification results, and yet it is also more computationally efficient than the other accurate state-of-the-art methods.

3.4.5 Discussion

By analysing the results provided by all the techniques above on the three considered datasets, one can see that the classification results of the LCKSVD is worst as it does not conisder any spatial information of the pixels. The SBDSM, JSM-DKSVD and SLAP, which all used a single scale window to gather contextual information, provided significantly higher classification accuracies than the

LCKSVD, but lower than the DSDL and CASRC which uses multiscale windows. Although, DSDL is able to provide good classification results, it is more sensitive to the segmentation method used to generate the superpixel images. For example, in Indian Pines dataset, the $\overline{OA}$ of DSDL decreased significantly when ISLIC is used in place of SLIC. This is also the case in Pavia University dataset, where the $\overline{AA}$ of DSDL increased significantly when ISLIC is used in place of SLIC. Moreover, the classification results from DSDL are inconsistent. For example, in Pavia University dataset, the DSDL provides high $\overline{OA}$ but low $\overline{AA}$ that indicates its failure to classify certain classes properly. On the other hand, thanks to the multiscale context-sensitive spectral features extracted, the proposed technique not only provides the best classification results, but it also provides consistent results irrespective of the segmentation method used and the datasets considered. Furthermore, the proposed technique is computationally more efficient than the best state-of-the-art techniques in the literature.

3.5 Conclusion

The success of sparse representation-based classifiers is dependent on the dictionaries they use. However, generating a compact, discriminative and representative dictionary is a challenging task. In this chapter, we proposed a method that extracts novel multiscale context-sensitive spectral features to be used for dictionary learning. Our method first uses superpixels and a fixed window to identify the appropriate spatial neighbourhoods of the pixel. Then, considering the spatial neighbourhoods of the pixel, SVD is used to extract the context-sensitive spectral features of it. The extracted features are finally used to learn the dictionaries for the classification of HSI.

The effectiveness of the proposed technique rigorously evaluated through a comparative analysis with six state-of-the-art methods across three HSI datasets. The experimental results consistently demonstrate that, in contrast to the state-of-the-art techniques, the proposed method yielded the best and most consistent performance across all considered datasets. One limitation of the proposed method is that the multiscale CSSF cannot be fused together to be used as a single feature set for classification as the number of features in each CSSF is very high (i.e. it is equal to the number of HSI bands). Therefore, developing a method to overcome this limitation could be a promising area for future research.

Chapter 4

Multiscale rank-1 spectral spatial features for hyperspectral image classification

4.1 Introduction

In the previous chapter, it was observed that the spectral-spatial features generated by exploiting the singular value decomposition (SVD) have good class representation and discrimination. However, its one limitation was that the features obtained from each scale could not be fused together as a single feature set for classification, since the combined features would have a very high dimensionality. Therefore, research was conducted to overcome the above challenges and in this thesis a novel SVD-based spectral-spatial feature extraction method was developed. In contrast to the first and second methods, here multiple fixed-size windows of increasing size are used to define spatial neighbourhoods of each pixel, following a dimensionality reduction process. Then, using the spatial contextual information obtained from them, more effective spectral-spatial features were generated and integrated. This approach not only addresses the dimensionality challenge but also enhances overall classification performance.

In the literature, several feature extraction techniques are proposed which extract spectral-spatial features of the pixels by considering its spatial information. Wavelet transform is one popular mathematical tool used to extract spectral-spatial features of the pixels in HSIs [227]. Other techniques such as Multiscale Superpixel Structural Profile (MSSP) [236], Band-by-Band Adaptive Multiscale Superpixel Feature Extraction (BAMS-FE) [124] exploit superpixels to extract spectral-spatial features. A large number of techniques incorporate spatial information of the pixel by considering the geometric shape of the object to which it belongs. Differential morphological profiles (DMPs) is one such approach, which captures the object's structures by using a structuring element of different sizes [4, 10]. Due to the static shape of the structuring elements, it may not be suitable for images having objects with diverse geometric shapes. To address this limitation, Extended Morphological Attribute Profiles (EMAPs) and Extended Extinction Profiles (EEPs) are proposed [11, 39, 58, 133]. Apart from morphological techniques, filtering methods like Gabor Filters (GFs), Edge Preserving Filters (EPFs) are also employed for spectral-spatial feature extraction [32, 107, 172]. Such filters incorporate spatial information by reducing noise and enhancing fine details present in the HSI. Some methods extract spectral-spatial features of the pixels by exploiting the textural information of the HSI. Local Binary Pattern (LBP) is one of such methods that has been used for HSI classification [33, 128, 233, 271]. In recent years, a number of deep learning models such as 2D-CNN [132], 3D-CNN [2], Hybrid CNN [22], EXNet [71] and AGCN [99] have been developed to extract spectral-spatial features in HSI. However, deep learning models are computationally demanding and need a large amount of labelled samples for training, which are not available in many remote sensing applications. From the literature, it is evident that spectral-spatial features play an important role for enhancing the classification results of HSIs. The main goal of these methods is to extract better features by suppressing the noise contamination of pixels while simultaneously emphasizing relevant spatial information through local spatial relationships among pixel. However, due to the high spatial and spectral complexity of the HSI, this objective is still difficult to achieve by the current state-of-the-art. Hence, the development of robust spectral-spatial feature extraction techniques still remains an ongoing research.

Therefore, building on the the significance of spectral-spatial information fusion and addressing the continuous need for effective feature extraction in HSI, we propose a method that exploits SVD to extract discriminant spectral-spatial features. The proposed method begins with a reduction in the dimensionality of the original HSI through PCA, retaining only the first few principal components (PCs). Subsequently, for each pixel, SVD is applied to approximate the information contained within a fixed-size neighborhood window. The approximated features with the central pixel of this window (called rank-1 spectral-spatial features (RSSF)) are used to represent the pixel. However, as a fixed-size window cannot capture sufficient spectral-spatial information, multiple fixed-size windows at different scales are used to extract multiple RSSF of the pixels. Finally, these RSSFs are stacked together to generate the MRSSF of the pixels for classification. The experiments carried out on four real benchmark hyperspectral datasets demonstrate the effectiveness of the proposed technique.

The chapter is organized as follows. The proposed method is presented in detail in Section 4.2.The experimental results and analysis are reported in Section 4.3. Finally, Section 4.4 gives the concluding remarks.

4.2 Proposed Method

The fusion of spatial and spectral information plays an important role in improving the classification results of HSIs. Our method exploits SVD to extract multiscale rank-1 spectral-spatial features (MRSSF) from the HSI. The pixels represented with MRSSF are classified using the kernel joint sparse representation classifier (KJSRC). The subsequent sections provide the details of the proposed methods.

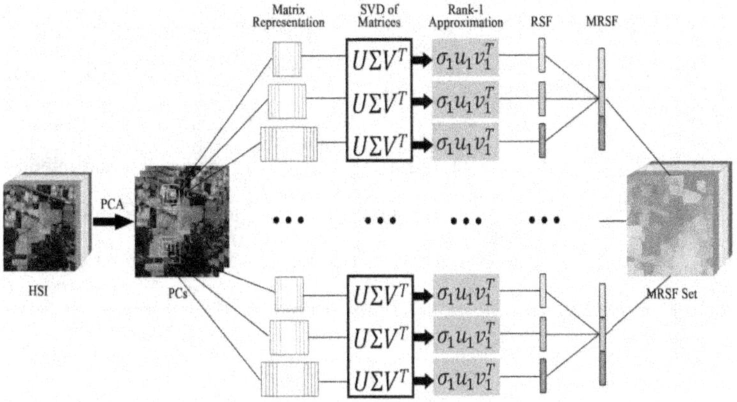

Figure 4-1: Overall framework of the proposed method for extracting MRSSF associated to each pixel in HSI.

4.2.1 Extraction of rank-1 spectral-spatial features (RSSF)

In this research, a technique is proposed that extracts features to represent the pixels in HSI by fusing spectral and spatial information. To extract such features, our technique exploits SVD. Initially, PCA is applied to construct a lower-dimensional image from the high-dimensional HSI by selecting only the first few PCs of it. Then for each pixel, considering it as a center of a fixed-size window in the lower-dimensional image, SVD is applied to approximate the information content of the pixels within the window. Then the extracted approximate features, which are called rank-1 spectral-spatial features (RSSF), are used to represent the center pixel.

In greater detail, given HSI $\mathbf{H} \in R^{P \times Q \times B}$, where $P \times Q$ denote the image's size and B the number of bands, our proposed technique generates a lower-dimensional image $\mathrm{I} \in R^{P \times Q \times l}$ by selecting first $l (l < B)$ PCs of the HSI. For a pixel $x \in \mathrm{I}$, considering it as the center pixel of a fixed-size $s \times s$ window J, the matrix $\mathrm{E_x}$ of size $l \times s^2$ is generated to store spectral values of all pixels within J. In order to extract spectral-spatial features of x, SVD is applied to the matrix $\mathrm{E_x}$ to decompose it into the matrices $\mathrm{U_x}, \Sigma_\mathrm{x}$ and $\mathrm{V_x}$ such that $\mathrm{E_x} = \mathrm{U_x}\Sigma_\mathrm{x}\mathrm{V_x}^T$. Here, $\mathrm{U_x}$ and $\mathrm{V_x}$ are the orthonormal matrices of sizes $l \times l$ and $s^2 \times s^2$, respectively, while Σ_x is a $l \times s^2$ diagonal matrix. Given that the rank of the matrix $\mathrm{E_x}$ is r, the first r column vectors of $\mathrm{U_x}$ (i.e., $u_1, u_2, ..., u_r$) and $\mathrm{V_x}$ (i.e., $\mathrm{v_1, v_2, ..., v_r}$) span the column and row space of $\mathrm{E_x}$ respectively. The first r nonzero decreasing diagonal elements of Σ_x (i.e., $\sigma_1 > \sigma_2, ..., \sigma_{r-1} > \sigma_r > 0$) show the importance of the different column vectors of $\mathrm{U_x}$ and $\mathrm{V_x}$ to reconstruct the matrix $\mathrm{E_x}$. Thus, the matrix $\mathrm{E_x}$ can be represented as a sum of r rank-1 matrices as follows:

$$\mathrm{E_x} = \mathrm{U_x}\Sigma_\mathrm{x}\mathrm{V_x}^T = \sigma_1 \mathrm{u_1 v_1^T} + \sigma_2 \mathrm{u_2 v_2^T} + ... + \sigma_r \mathrm{u}_r \mathrm{v}_r^T. \tag{4.1}$$

Where the importance of the $1^{st}, 2^{nd}, ...r^{th}$ rank-1 matrices gradually decreases to reconstruct the $\mathrm{E_x}$. As the rank-1 matrix $\sigma_1 \mathrm{u_1 v_1}^\mathrm{T}$ keeps maximum information of $\mathrm{E_x}$, in this work $\mathrm{E_x}$ is approximated as:

$$\mathrm{E_x} \approx \sigma_1 \mathrm{u_1 v_1^T}. \tag{4.2}$$

Note that each column (feature vector) of the matrix $\sigma_1 \mathrm{u_1 v_1^T}$ is associated with a pixel inside the window J and is obtained by considering the spectral information of all pixels within the window J. Thus, the components of the column vector (feature vector) of the rank-1 matrix $\sigma_1 \mathrm{u_1 v_1^T}$ associated with the center pixel x consider both spectral and spatial information to represent it in a l-dimensional feature space. The derived rank-1 spectral-spatial feature (RSSF) of x is denoted as x_{RSSF}.

4.2.2 Generation of multiscale RSSF (MRSSF)

As mentioned above, the RSSF for a pixel x is extracted considering its spatial neighbourhood, which is defined by using a fixed-size window J. As the shape of the objects in HSI follows different structures and dimensions, this fixed-sized window does not provide sufficient spatial information for modeling the pixels. To better represent the spatial information of a pixel $x \in \mathrm{I}$, multiple windows of increasing size are selected instead of considering a single window J. Then, for each window, x_{RSSF} is extracted. The RSSF extracted for each window are stacked together to generate a multiscale RSSF (MRSSF) of x:

$$x_{MRSSF} = \{x_{RSSF_1}; x_{RSSF_2}; \ldots; x_{RSSF_g}\} \tag{4.3}$$

where g is the number of windows considered, and thus x_{MRSSF} consists of $g \times l$ features. The steps to generate the MRSSF for each pixel in the HSI are shown in Figure 4-1 and algorithm 4. Since MRSSF is generated by considering spectral information of the neighbouring pixels, it provides better information to discriminate different objects in HSI.

4.2.3 Classification of HSI

After representing each pixel $x \in$ H with x_{MRSSF} in the feature space R^{lg}, the Kernel Joint Sparse Representation Classifier (KJSRC), which is an extension of the Joint Sparse Representation Classifier (JSRC) is used to classify unknown pixels. To classify an unknown pixel $y \in \mathbf{H}$ represented with the feature vector y_{MRSSF}, JSRC assumes that the feature vectors of neighboring pixels can be represented by a linear combination of the same dictionary atoms. Hence, they share the same sparsity pattern in their sparse vectors but with different coefficients. Let Y be the matrix containing the feature vectors of y and its neighbouring pixels, then its sparse representation matrix A can be expressed as:

$$\hat{\mathrm{A}} = \arg\min_{\mathrm{A}} \|\mathrm{Y} - \mathrm{DA}\|_{\mathrm{F}} \quad s.t. \; \|\mathrm{A}\|_{row,0} < K \tag{4.4}$$

where K is sparsity level of sparsity, $\|\mathrm{A}\|_{row,0}$ the number of non-zero rows of A that control sparsity, and $\|.\|_F$ represents the Frobenius norm. In KJSRC, the kernel function $\Phi : \mathcal{X} \rightarrow \mathcal{F}$ projects the pixels from their original feature space to a higher dimensional kernel space. In this space, the dictionary D is expressed as $\mathrm{V}' = [\Phi(d_1), \Phi(d_2), \ldots, \Phi(d_N)]$ and Y as $\Phi(\mathrm{Y})$, where d_i represents the atom and

Algorithm 4 Proposed MRSSF

```
Input: Hyperspectral Image H; sparsity level K; window's sizes [s_1 × s_1, s_2 × s_2, ..., s_g × s_g]

//Extract MRSSF
From HSI H construct I by considering first l PCs
for each pixel x ∈ I do
    for i=1 to g do
        Consider x as center pixel of a fixed-size s_i × s_i window J
        Store the spectral features of the pixels within J into a matrix E_x^i
        Apply SVD to decompose E_x^i into U_x Σ_x V_x^T
        Approximate E_x^i using rank-1 matrix as E_x^i ≈ σ_1 u_1 v_1^T
        x_{RSSF_i} = the column vector of σ_1 u_1 v_1^T associated to x
    end for
    x_{MRSSF} = {x_{RSSF_1}; x_{RSSF_2}; ...; x_{RSSF_g}}
end for
//Classification
for each unlabelled pixel y ∈ I do
    Compute the sparse coefficient Â' of Φ(Y) by using Equation (4.5)
    Assign class label of pixel y by predicting the class label of y_MRSSF using
    Equation (4.7)
end for
```

N is the total number of atoms in the dictionary. Thus, Equation (4.4) can be written as follows:

$$\hat{\mathrm{A}}' = \arg\min_{\mathrm{A}'} \|\Phi(\mathrm{Y}) - \mathrm{V}'\mathrm{A}'\|_{\mathrm{F}} \quad s.t. \ \|\mathrm{A}'\|_{row,0} < K \tag{4.5}$$

For each of the C classes considered, the reconstruction error between $\Phi(\mathrm{Y})$ and its approximation is computed. The class that provides the smallest reconstruction error is assigned to the unknown pattern y_{MRSSF} as follows:

$$f(\mathrm{y_{MRSSF}}) = \|\Phi(\mathrm{Y}) - \mathrm{V}'_{\mathrm{i}}\hat{\mathrm{A}}'_{\mathrm{i}}\|_F \quad for\ i = 1, 2, \ldots, C \tag{4.6}$$

$$\hat{c} = \arg\min_{i=1,2,\ldots,C}\{f(\mathrm{y_{MRSSF}})\} \tag{4.7}$$

4.3 Experimental Results

The details of the experimental setup and the results obtained by the different techniques are presented below.

4.3.1 Experimental Setup

In order to assess the proposed technique's effectiveness, four widely recognized hyperspectral datasets – namely, University of Pavia, University of Houston 2013, Indian Pines and University of Houston 2018 are used. The description of each of these datasets is given in Appendix A. The classification performance of the proposed technique are compared with those provided by representing the pixels with several state-of-the-art spectral-spatial features, including Differential Morphological Profile (DMP) [4], Extended Morphological Attribute Profile (EMAP) [39], Principal Component Anaysis based Edge Preserving Filters (PCA-EPFs) [107], Local Binary Pattern for Sparse Representation using Product Moment Correlation (LBP-SRPMC) [33], Structure Profile (SP) [52] and Band-by-band adaptive multiscale superpixel feature extraction (BAMS-FE) [124]. For PCA-EPFs, LBP-SRPMC, SP and BAMS-FE, the parameter settings given in the corresponding publications are used. For DMP and MRSSF, windows ranging from 5×5 to 25×25 with a step increment of 2 are considered and first 15 PCs are used to generate them. This number of PCs has been derived according to an emperical experimental analysis. In EMAP, *area* attribute with multiple thresholds is used to construct the profile. For a fair comparison, the spectral-spatial features extracted by different techniques, including our proposed one, are classified using the same classifier i.e., the KJSRC classifier by considering a 3×3 window, $\gamma = 2^7$ and the sparsity level $K = 30$. Furthermore, our proposed technique is compared with many deep learning based techniques.

The effect of the proposed technique was assessed through three sets of experiments. In the first set, our proposed MRSSF was compared against several state-of-the-art spectral-spatial features using stratified sampling strategy for selecting training and testing sets. The second set of experiments standard training and test datasets, as suggested by the remote sensing community [69]. Note that for the University of Houston 2018 dataset, this experiment is not performed due to the unavailability of standard training and test sets. The third set of experiments aimed to demonstrate the robustness of the proposed technique by evaluating its performance across varying numbers of labelled (training) samples. The performance of all methods in these experiments was quantitatively measured using overall accuracy (OA), average accuracy (AA) and Kappa accuracy (κ). All the experiments are implemented in 64 bit Matlab environment and executed on a personal computer with 64-bit operating system, Intel(R) Core(TM) i5-10500 CPU clocked at 3.10GHz, and 24 GB of RAM.

Table 4.1: Training and Testing Samples for the Pavia University and University of Houston 2018 datasets.

Pavia University			University of Houston 2018		
Name	Training Sample	Testing Sample	Name	Training Sample	Testing Sample
Asphalt	200	6381	Grass Healthy	136	1217
Meadows	200	18399	Grass Stresses	489	4399
Gravel	200	1849	Trees	277	2489
Broad Trees	200	2814	Water	5	17
PMS	200	1095	Residential	535	4812
Bare Soil	200	4779	Non-Residential	3246	29213
Bitumen	200	1080	Road	637	5728
SBB	200	3432			
Shadows	200	697			

4.3.2 Results

In real case scenario, limited number of training samples are available. Therefore, in the experiment, we choose to select only a tiny portion of the total samples for training and the rest are used for testing. Table 4.1 and Table 4.2 shows the different number of training and testing samples for each dataset. To validate the effectiveness of the proposed MRSSF, different experiments are performed on these four benchmark datasets. The analysis of the results of these experiments

Table 4.2: Training and Testing Samples for University of Houston 2013 and Indian Pines datasets.

University of Houston 2013			Indian Pines		
Name	**Training Sample**	**Testing Sample**	**Name**	**Training Sample**	**Testing Sample**
Grass Healthy	126	1125	Alfalfa	5	41
Grass Stresses	126	1128	Corn-Notill	143	1285
Grass Synthetic	70	627	Corn-Mintill	83	747
Tree	125	1119	Corn	24	213
Soil	125	1119	Grass-Pasture	48	435
Water	33	292	Grass-Trees	73	657
Residential	127	1141	Grs-Pas-Mow	3	25
Commercial	125	1119	Hay-Windrowed	48	430
Road	126	1126	Oats	2	18
Highway	123	1104	Soyabean-Notill	97	875
Railway	124	1111	Soyabean-Mintill	246	2209
Parking Lot 1	124	1109	Soyabean Clean	59	534
Parking Lot 2	47	422	Wheat	21	184
Tennis Court	43	385	Woods	127	1138
Running Track	66	594	B-G-T-D	40	347
			Stone-Steel-Towers	9	84

are presented in the next subsections.

Results: University of Pavia Dataset

For the first experiment conducted on the University of Pavia dataset, 200 labelled samples from each class are randomly selected for training and the rest are used for testing. The experiment is run five times, and the average classification results provided by the KJSRC classifier are computed for different feature sets. Table 4.3 reports the average accuracy obtained by the spectral features, DMP, EMAP, PCA-EPFs, LBP-SRPMC, SP, BAMS-FE and proposed MRSSF. From this table, it can be observed that the proposed MRSSF provides better results with an $\overline{OA}$ of 99.28% and $\overline{AA}$ of 99.36%, compared to the other existing feature sets. Fig 4-2 shows the classification maps obtained by different techniques. From the figure, one can see that the PCA-EPFs, SP and our proposed MRSSF provided smoother classification maps than the rest.

Table 4.3: Classification results provided by the KJSRC considering the original spectral feature, DMP, EMAP, PCA-EPFs, LBP-SRPMC, SP, BAMS-FE and the proposed MRSSF (University of Pavia dataset).

Class No.	Spectral	DMP	EMAP	PCA-EPFs	LBP-SRPMC	SP	BAMS-FE	Proposed MRSSF
Experiment 1: Randomly Chosen Training and Test Sets (five runs)								
1	99.43	94.38	91.14	97.66	54.15	97.46	99.82	97.69
2	99.34	96.55	93.87	99.29	67.67	98.34	99.05	99.73
3	100	97.04	94.31	99.34	87.74	99.14	99.73	99.66
4	100	97.72	98.91	95.74	93.77	93.92	94.72	99.25
5	99.87	99.77	99.95	100	100	100	99.91	100
6	95.48	97.55	95.05	100	88.30	99.94	99.86	99.93
7	96.99	98.87	97.88	99.93	98.37	99.49	100	100
8	94.19	95.96	93.03	99.05	80.10	98.11	99.62	98.21
9	93.25	99.76	100	99.09	99.12	99.65	99.61	99.81
$\overline{OA}$	96.69 ±0.52	96.59 ±0.57	94.27 ±0.48	98.88 ±0.24	74.11 ±1.08	98.20 ±0.50	99.08 ±0.15	**99.28** ±0.08
$\overline{AA}$	95.99 ±0.92	97.51 ±0.14	96.01 ±0.19	98.89 ±0.21	85.46 ±0.22	98.44 ±0.21	99.03 ±0.21	**99.36** ±0.12
$\overline{\kappa}$	0.96 ±0	0.95 ±0	0.92 ±0	0.98 ±0	0.68 ±0.01	0.98 ±0	**0.99** ±0	**0.99** ±0
Experiment 2: Standard Training and Test Sets								
OA	79.43	77.37	82.94	85.81	53.35	74.21	86.53	**91.25**
AA	83.33	88.03	87.51	85.86	61.84	81.51	85.44	**93.24**
κ	0.78	0.72	0.78	0.81	0.43	0.67	0.86	**0.88**

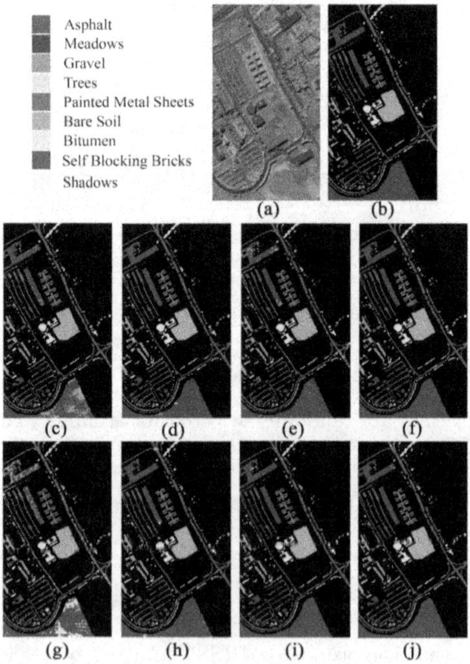

Figure 4-2: a) False color decomposition of Pavia University image, and b) its ground truth map. The classification maps produced by the KJSRC by considering c) Spectral feature, d) DMP, e) EMAP, f) PCA-EPFs, g) LBP-SRPMC, h) SP, i) BAMS-FE, and j) Proposed MRSSF

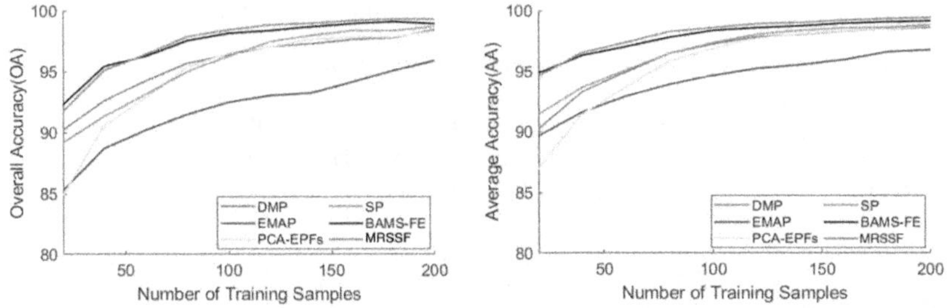

Figure 4-3: OA and AA of KJSRC across different feature sets versus different training sample sizes (Pavia University dataset).

In the second experiment, the standard training and test sets of University of Pavia are used for comparison. Table 4.3 also reports the classification results of the different techniques using the standard training and test sets. From the table, one can see that there is a significant improvement in OA and AA. The proposed MRSSF provided an OA of 91.25% and an AA of 93.24% that are approximately 5% higher than the value obtained by the best literature feature set (BAMS-FE). This shows the robustness of the MRSSF in effectively capturing the spectral-spatial information of the pixels in HSI.

Finally, the results of the third experiment shown in Figure 4-3, point out that the proposed MRSSF exhibits better OA and AA regardless of the number of labelled samples used to train the classifier. This again validate the robustness of the proposed MRSSF to incorporate better spectral-spatial information compared to the other state-of-the-art feature sets.

Results: University of Houston 2013

For this dataset, 10% of labelled samples from each class are randomly selected for training and the rest 90% are used for testing. Table 4.4 reports the accuracies obtained by the different techniques for five runs. From the table, one can see that again, our proposed MRSSF method provides the highest accuracy. It produces an $\overline{OA}$ of 98.85% and $\overline{AA}$ of 98.67%, which are higher values than EMAP (which is the most accurate literature technique) with an $\overline{OA}$ of 97.92 and $\overline{AA}$ of 97.13. The classification maps produced by different techniques are shown in Figure 4-

4. This figure illustrates that the proposed technique incorporates better spatial information compared to the other state-of-the-art methods.

Table 4.4: Classification results provided by the KJSRC considering the original spectral feature, DMP, EMAP, PCA-EPFs, LBP-SRPMC, SP, BAMS-FE and the proposed MRSSF (University of Houston 2013 dataset).

Experiment 1: Randomly Chosen Training and Test Sets (five runs)								
Class No.	**Spectral**	**DMP**	**EMAP**	**PCA-EPFs**	**LBP-SRPMC**	**SP**	BAMS-FE	**Proposed MRSSF**
1	99.34	98.99	99.68	99.11	99.75	98.81	97.80	99.02
2	99.26	96.24	99.27	97.66	99.11	95.05	96.38	99.96
3	100	99.62	99.97	99.97	100	99.71	100	100
4	100	99.12	99.66	94.28	99.98	92.48	93.42	99.73
5	99.89	98.57	99.77	100	99.66	99.89	100	99.86
6	98.42	91.58	99.04	95.68	96.37	83.08	93.97	96.37
7	97.84	97.35	98.30	93.46	97.56	90.83	89.75	97.93
8	96.87	92.62	98.19	96.80	96.01	96.18	92.78	98.23
9	92.54	97.98	95.68	92.91	93.00	91.79	94.35	97.89
10	97.19	98.95	99.57	99.86	96.68	99.11	99.47	98.84
11	94.58	98.97	98.52	99.64	93.12	98.42	99.10	99.19
12	96.43	97.73	97.04	97.26	94.39	98.77	98.03	98.52
13	76.92	76.87	72.80	97.54	77.77	93.27	92.99	94.69
14	100	99.32	99.48	100	100	99.06	99.95	100
15	99.73	99.39	100	100	99.66	100	99.33	99.93
$\overline{OA}$	97.07 ±0.34	97.08 ±0.31	97.92 ±0.45	97.41 ±0.46	96.67 ±0.12	96.16 ±0.50	96.37 ±0.30	**98.85** ±0.45
$\overline{AA}$	96.60±0.33	96.22 ±0.37	97.13 ±0.57	97.61 ±0.60	96.20 ±0.22	95.76 ±0.33	96.48 ±0.22	**98.67** ±0.43
$\overline{\kappa}$	0.97±0	0.97 ±0	0.98±0	0.97±0	0.96±0	0.96 ±0	0.96 ±0	**0.99**±0
Experiment 2: Standard Training and Test Sets								
OA	79.43	69.98	81.84	64.67	78.48	62.64	66.30	**82.38**
AA	83.33	74.01	84.49	70.57	80.83	68.58	71.55	**85.31**
κ	0.78	0.67	0.80	0.62	0.77	0.59	0.63	**0.81**

In the second experiment, the standard training and test sets of the University of Houston 2013 dataset were used for comparative evaluation. Table 4.4 presents the classification results obtained by the various techniques using these standard data sets. The table reveals that the proposed technique again demonstrates superior performance on this dataset, achieving an OA of 82.38%, and an AA of 85.31%. This outcome provides further validation of the effectiveness of the proposed MRSSF in capturing enhanced spectral-spatial information from the pixels in HSI.

As in the previous case of the Pavia University dataset, also in this case the proposed MRSSF performs comparatively better than the other state-of-the-art methods for different numbers of labelled samples, as shown in Figure 4-5. This further highlights the robustness and potentiality of the proposed method to obtain better discriminatory features over the other methods.

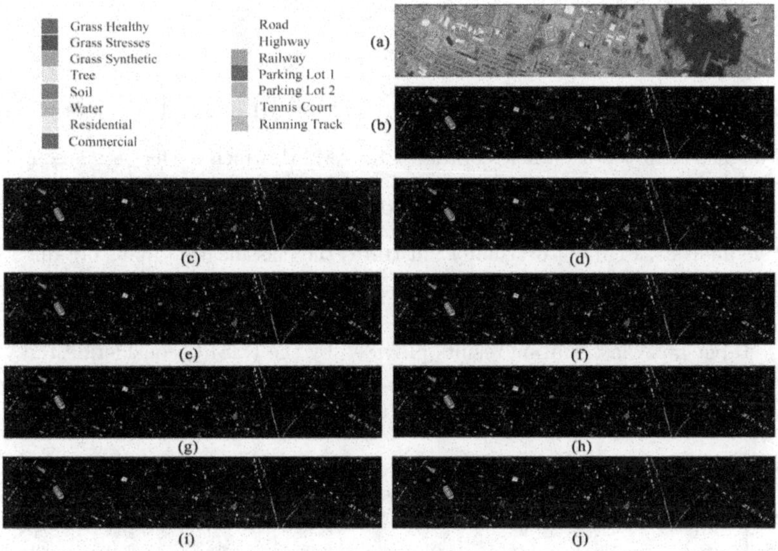

Figure 4-4: a) False color decomposition of University of Houston 2013 image, and b) its ground truth map. The classification maps produced by the KJSRC by considering c) Spectral feature, d) DMP, e) EMAP, f) PCA-EPFs, g) LBP-SRPMC, h) SP, i) BAMS-FE, and j) Proposed MRSSF

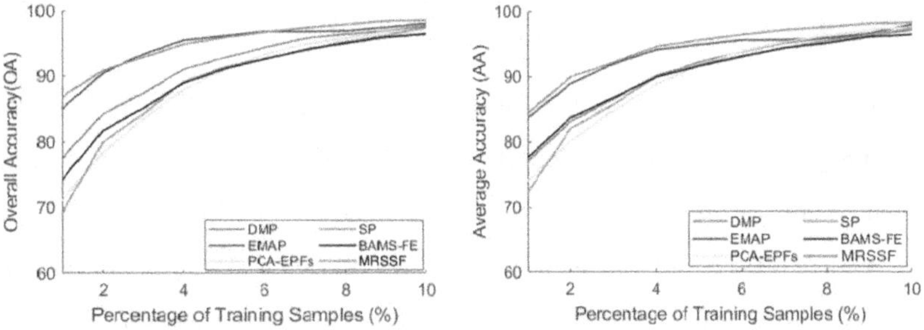

Figure 4-5: OA and AA of KJSRC across different feature sets versus different training sample sizes (University of Houston 2013 dataset).

Results: University of Houston 2018

Similar to the University of Houston 2013 dataset, 10% of labelled samples from each class of this dataset are randomly selected for training and the rest 90% are used for testing. The experiment is run five times, and the average classification results provided by KJSRC for different feature sets are computed. Table 4.5 reports the average classification accuracies obtained by the different feature extraction techniques. From this table, one can see that even for this dataset the proposed technique provides significantly better results than all other methods considered. It produces an $\overline{OA}$ of 97.76 and an $\overline{AA}$ of 94.44 which is at least 2% higher than the accuracies obtained by EMAP, which is the best among the state-of-the-art technique, with an $\overline{OA}$ of 95.78 and an $\overline{AA}$ of 91.52. For qualitative analysis, Figure 4-6 visually illustrates the classification maps obtained by different techniques.

Table 4.5: Classification results provided by the KJSRC considering the original spectral feature, DMP, EMAP, PCA-EPFs, LBP-SRPMC, SP, BAMS-FE and the proposed MRSSF (University of Houston 2018 dataset).

Experiment 1: Randomly Chosen Training and Test Sets (five runs)								
Class No.	**Spectral**	**DMP**	**EMAP**	**PCA-EPFs**	**LBP-SRPMC**	**SP**	BAMS-FE	**Proposed MRSSF**
1	83.68	79.72	79.54	73.05	65.19	72.67	80.54	76.81
2	96.13	93.04	94.84	90.93	92.68	88.89	85.41	94.69
3	90.42	93.86	91.24	88.01	74.72	84.92	91.99	95.87
4	100.00	84.71	92.94	85.88	65.88	81.88	85.88	100.00
5	85.08	96.62	93.37	98.44	83.50	97.84	97.89	99.12
6	98.20	98.56	98.48	99.14	99.38	98.39	98.59	99.57
7	86.18	86.44	90.25	84.72	45.46	85.60	89.07	95.04
$\overline{OA}$	94.47 ±0.13	95.67 ±0.12	95.78 ±0.06	95.34 ±0.16	88.55 ±0.25	94.56 ±0.18	95.36 ±0.10	**97.76** ±0.02
$\overline{AA}$	91.38 ±0.27	90.42 ±2.49	91.52 ±1.32	88.59 ±1.54	75.26 ±2.51	87.06 ±4.04	89.21 ±2.14	**94.44** ±0.25
$\overline{\kappa}$	0.91 ±0	0.93 ±0	0.93 ±0	0.92 ±0	0.79 ±0	0.91 ±0	0.93 ±0	**0.96** ±0

Since there are no standard training and test sets, we could not perform the second experiment for this dataset. However, the results of the third experiment, presented in Figure 4-7, reveal that the proposed method consistently outperforms all considered state-of-the-art feature sets across varying numbers of labeled samples. This provides further evidence of the effectiveness of the proposed MRSSF.

Results: Indian Pines

Lastly, for this dataset, 10% of labelled samples from each class are randomly selected for training and the rest 90% are used for testing. Table 4.6 reports the average of OA, AA and κ obtained by the different techniques for five runs. From the table, one can see that the results obtained by our proposed MRSSF method are comparable with that of the best method (BAMS-FE) in the literature. It produces an $\overline{OA}$ of 98.39% and $\overline{AA}$ of 96.22%, while BAMS-FE produces an $\overline{OA}$

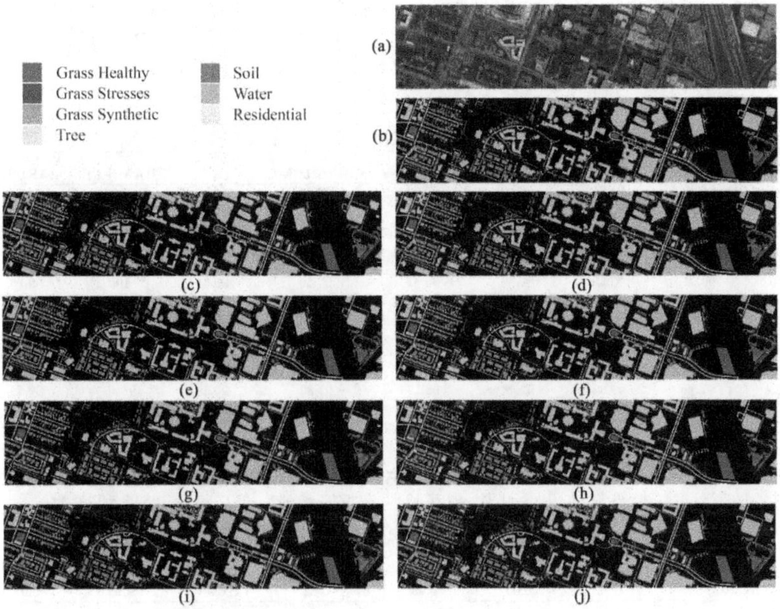

Figure 4-6: a) False color decomposition of University of Houston 2018 image, and b) its ground truth map. The classification maps produced by the KJSRC considering c) Spectral feature, d) DMP, e) EMAP, f) PCA-EPFs, g) LBP-SRPMC, h) SP, i) BAMS-FE, and j) Proposed MRSSF

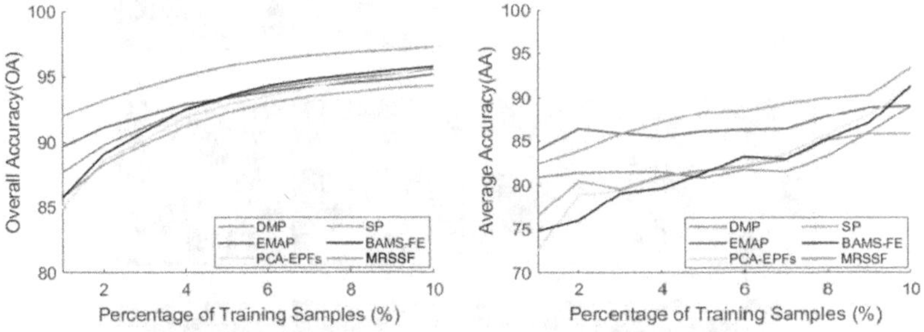

Figure 4-7: OA and AA of KJSRC across different feature sets versus different training sample sizes (University of Houston 2018 dataset).

of 98.93 and $\overline{AA}$ of 98.99. For qualitative analysis, the classification maps produced by different techniques are shown in Figure 4-8.

In the second experiment, the standard training and test sets from the Indian Pines dataset are used for comparison. Table 4.6 also reports the classification results obtained by the different techniques using the standard training and test

Table 4.6: Classification results provided by the KJSRC considering the original spectral feature, DMP, EMAP, PCA-EPFs, LBP-SRPMC, SP, BAMS-FE and the proposed MRSSF (Indian Pines dataset).

Class No.	Spectral	DMP	EMAP	PCA-EPFs	LBP-SRPMC	SP	BAMS-FE	Proposed MRSSF
	Experiment 1: Randomly Chosen Training and Test Sets (five runs)							
1	65.85	91.71	96.10	87.32	82.44	84.88	98.05	94.63
2	86.71	98.97	94.32	98.41	94.37	96.78	97.74	96.14
3	85.73	98.50	98.13	98.50	92.85	97.97	99.04	98.69
4	85.07	98.03	92.68	98.12	97.56	94.65	98.59	95.68
5	95.03	95.26	94.07	98.34	91.45	94.85	98.76	96.83
6	99.54	96.59	99.88	96.41	96.56	99.54	100	99.76
7	88.00	100	91.20	99.20	74.40	96.00	97.60	98.40
8	99.77	100	100	99.21	97.95	99.49	100	100
9	20.00	81.11	61.11	16.67	42.22	56.67	100	64.78
10	85.55	99.02	93.92	99.41	90.51	97.74	96.96	98.22
11	94.40	98.90	98.57	99.25	97.95	98.57	99.24	99.12
12	85.32	93.86	92.36	98.13	93.82	95.58	98.46	97.42
13	99.24	98.59	99.57	99.35	95.22	99.89	99.78	99.02
14	98.40	99.88	99.84	99.96	99.51	99.75	99.98	99.81
15	81.91	98.38	99.08	98.90	97.28	96.65	100	99.60
16	98.81	100	94.76	97.14	71.43	97.86	99.76	98.57
$\overline{OA}$	91.56 ±0.74	98.32 ±0.34	97.00 ±0.11	98.59 ±0.23	93.80 ±0.59	97.80 ±0.34	**98.93** ±0.20	98.39 ±0.06
$\overline{AA}$	85.58±1.23	96.80 ±1.70	94.09 ±1.95	92.77 ±1.32	87.33 ±1.53	94.17 ±1.46	**98.99** ±0.20	96.22 ±0.79
$\overline{\kappa}$	0.90±0	0.98 ±0	0.97±0	0.98±0	0.93±0	0.97 ±0	**0.99** ±0	0.98±0
	Experiment 2: Standard Training and Test Sets							
OA	83.92	95.54	95.93	96.80	83.85	95.11	**97.67**	94.81
AA	91.82	96.82	92.65	93.97	91.76	91.86	**98.58**	96.83
κ	0.81	0.95	0.96	0.96	0.82	0.95	**0.97**	0.94

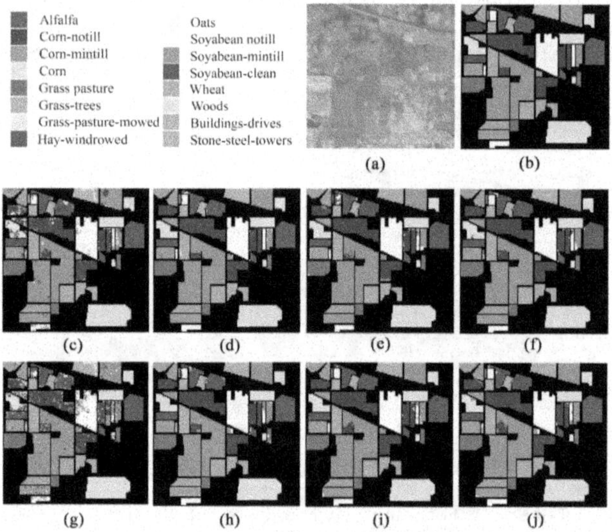

Figure 4-8: a) False color decomposition of Indian Pines image, and b) its ground truth map. The classification maps produced by the KJSRC by considering c) Spectral feature, d) DMP, e) EMAP, f) PCA-EPFs, g) LBP-SRPMC, h) SP, i) BAMS-FE, and j) Proposed MRSSF

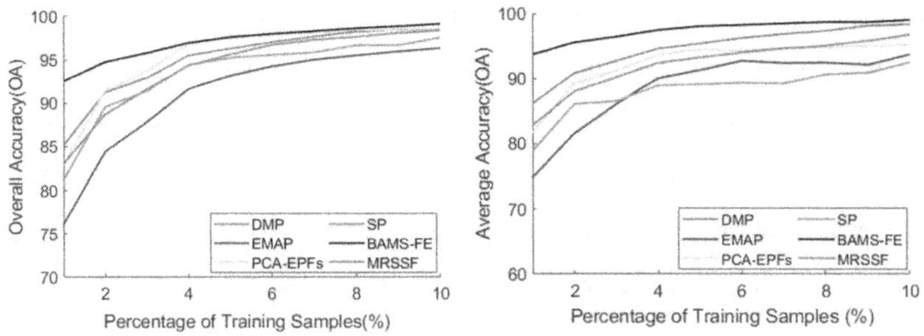

Figure 4-9: OA and AA of KJSRC across different feature sets versus different training sample sizes (Indian Pines dataset).

sets. From the table, one can see that the proposed technique provides an OA of 94.81%, and an AA of 96.83%.

For the third experiment, the performance of the proposed MRSSF in this experiment is comparatively lower than that of a few state-of-the-art methods, as shown in Figure 4-9. This is because most of the homogeneous regions in this dataset are small and since we have considered multiple large fixed-size windows for each pixel, many of these distinct regions are club together into one spatial neighbourhood. As a result, the features extracted from such neighbourhoods are less representative and discriminative, ultimately degrading the classification performance.

Results: Comparison with deep learning models

As mentioned before, deep learning models have become popular because of their ability to extract highly informative spatial features from hyperspectral images. In this section, to further demonstrate the effectiveness of our proposed method we benchmark our proposed method against state-of-the-art deep learning models. These models are 2D-CNN [132], 3D-CNN [2], Hybrid CNN [22], EXNet [99] and AGCN [71]. Note that after extracting the MRSSF from the hyperpsectral images, our proposed method utilizes the KJSRC for classification, which is simpler and computationally less expensive than deep learning models. Table 4.7 reports the OA, AA, and κ values obtained by considered methods for the above four HSI datasets. The results presented in the table indicate that our proposed method achieves higher performance than the deep learning models for the Pavia University, University of Houston 2018, and Indian Pines datasets with moderate execution time. Specifically, it produces an $\overline{OA}$ of 99.28% and $\overline{AA}$ of 99.36% for Pavia University, while the best among the deep learning models, the Hybrid CNN, could produce only an $\overline{OA}$ of 98.89% and $\overline{AA}$ of 98.94%. For the University of Houston 2018 dataset, the proposed method produces an $\overline{OA}$ of 97.76% and $\overline{AA}$ of 94.44%, which is higher than the best result produced by Hybrid CNN with an $\overline{OA}$ of 97.32% and $\overline{AA}$ of 92.42%. And for the Indian Pines dataset, the proposed method produces an $\overline{OA}$ of 98.27% and $\overline{AA}$ of 96.79% higher than all the other considered methods. Moreover, for the University of Houston 2013 dataset, our proposed model is able to produce results similar to the best literature model, with an $\overline{OA}$ of 98.85% and $\overline{AA}$ of 98.67%. In terms of execution time, our proposed method is much lower than that of the heavyweight ExNet model and comparable to the lightweight 2D-CNN and Hybrid CNN models. Note that the execution time of the proposed technique is heavily dependent on the generation of MRSSF that can be further reduced by optimizing our MATLAB code.

Discussion

By analysing the above results for four HSI datasets, it is evident that the spectral feature and LBP-SRPMC provide the lowest classification results among all feature sets. This indicates that LBP may not be a suitable tool for extracting spectral-spatial features of pixels in HSI. Moreover, SP and EMAP known for capturing good spectral-spatial information of the pixels, performed below par compared to the proposed MRSSF. Furthermore, other feature sets such as DMP, PCA-EPFs, and BAMS-FE produce good but inconsistent results. For example, BAMS-FE provides good result for the University of Pavia dataset ($\overline{OA}$ of 99.08%), but significantly poorer result for the University of Houston 2013($\overline{OA}$ of 96.37%) and University of Houston 2018 ($\overline{OA}$ of 95.36%) dataset. However, the proposed

Table 4.7: Classification results and computational time obtained by 2D-CNN, 3D-CNN, Hybrid CNN, ExNet, AGCN, and proposed MRSSF.

Dataset	Metrics	2D-CNN	3D-CNN	Hybrid CNN	ExNet	AGCN	Proposed MRSSF
Pavia University	$\overline{OA}$	96.20	98.03	98.89	97.92	88.36	**99.28**
	$\overline{AA}$	96.46	98.06	98.94	97.92	91.48	**99.36**
	$\overline{\kappa}$	0.95	0.97	0.98	0.97	0.85	**0.99**
	Time (s)	**76.92**	144.20	102.44	1631.55	177.95	108.61
Houston 2013	$\overline{OA}$	95.34	98.71	**98.85**	98.74	91.14	**98.85**
	$\overline{AA}$	91.07	98.59	98.83	98.75	91.07	**98.67**
	$\overline{\kappa}$	0.95	**0.99**	**0.99**	**0.99**	0.90	**0.99**
	Time (s)	**95.30**	256.60	143.60	1488.23	167.80	238.07
Houston 2018	$\overline{OA}$	96.30	95.56	97.32	96.89	96.35	**97.76**
	$\overline{AA}$	93.31	90.61	92.42	93.67	82.44	**94.44**
	κ	0.94	0.94	0.95	0.95	0.94	**0.96**
	Time (s)	**321.17**	899.88	491.28	5404.08	608.03	701.99
Indian Pines	$\overline{OA}$	89.70	93.70	97.50	95.87	79.06	**98.27**
	$\overline{AA}$	81.80	88.97	94.69	88.55	62.40	**96.79**
	$\overline{\kappa}$	0.88	0.93	0.97	0.95	0.76	**0.98**
	Time (s)	52.3	157.02	104.11	1065.04	119.25	**14.29**

MRSSF always provides better and consistent results than the other feature sets. Furthermore, the proposed method also performs better than several deep learning models. This is attributed to SVD's ability to incorporate better spectral and spatial information into the MRSSF, resulting in better discriminative capability.

4.4 Conclusion

Numerous techniques for extracting spectral-spatial features for HSI classification have been proposed in the literature. However, because of the low interclass and high intraclass variability of HSI, extraction of robust spectral-spatial features is still a challenging research issue. In this chapter, we proposed a method to extract novel spectral-spatial features of the pixels in HSI. Firstly, our proposed method reduces the dimensionality of the original HSI by considering only the first few PCs of it. Then, SVD is applied to the pixels within multiple fixed-size windows, to extract multiscale rank-1 spectral-spatial features of a given pixel. The proposed MRSSF is capable of capturing detailed spectral and spatial information of the pixel. As a result, it exhibits high discrimination and representation power. The effectiveness of the proposed MRSSF has been validated by comparing it with seven state-of-the-art feature sets and five deep learning models using four real HSI datasets. The experimental results show the superiority of the proposed MRSSF.

Chapter 5

Active Learning for Hyperspectral Image Classification Using Kernel Sparse Representation Classifiers

5.1 Introduction

The extraction and utilisation of spectral-spatial information has definitely aid in reducing the noise and enhancing the discrimination between pixels of different classes in HSI. However, supervised methods like sparse representation classification (SRC) would still require good and sufficient labelled samples to enhance the classification accuracy even further. Since the labelling of samples is costly and time-consuming, active learning methods were developed as a solution to this problem.

From the first chapter, it is learned that the fundamental step of AL is defining the query function that selects informative samples for labelling from the unlabeled pool. In batch mode AL, the query function is usually defined by combining uncertainty and diversity criteria. These uncertainty criteria are mostly supervised in nature, i.e., they are defined by exploiting the classifiers. In the literature, most of the AL techniques exploit support vector machines (SVM) classifier for defining uncertainty criterion because of its classification rule characterized by a small set of support vectors (SV). Some popular and widely used uncertainty criteria are marginal sampling (MS) [148, 225], multiclass level uncertainty (MCLU) [47], entropy query-by-bagging (EQB) [225], cluster assumption based histogram thresholding (CAHT) [162] and breaking tie (BT) [160]. Note that BT criterion is conceptually the same as MCLU criterion except that the first is more generalized (i.e., it can be defined by exploiting any classifiers), whereas the latter is defined by exploiting the one-against-all SVM classifier.

Since the uncertain samples selected by applying the above AL criterion may have redundancy. Therefore, both an uncertainty and a diversity criterion are applied in order to select informative (i.e., uncertain and non-redundant) samples. In [19], angular based diversity (ABD) is applied to select diverse samples from the selected uncertain samples by maximizing their angle in the spectral domain. The closest support vector (cSV) is another diversity defined using the SVM classifier [225]. It selects a subset of the most uncertain samples that exhibit the minimum distance to distinct support vectors identified by the SVM. Clustering based diversity are also widely used in AL. K-means, kernel k-means, self organizing map (SOM) are the clustering techniques used to select diverse samples [47, 164]. In recent years, other advanced AL techniques have been proposed in the literature [153, 165, 188, 245].However, the query functions of most of these techniques still rely on the above-mentioned criteria. Therefore, improvement of these criteria (especially of the uncertainty criterion) by exploiting a suitable classifier is the main motivation of this research.

Sparse representation classifier has proven to be a robust classifier and although several advancements have been made in recent years, yet it is rarely applied in the context of active learning. Huo et al. [95] tried to used SRC to define the BT uncertainty criterion for HSI classification, but their model failed to get convincing results. In [234], Wang et al. applied sparse modelling to select diverse uncertain samples, but they relied on the SVM-based uncertainty criterion.

Therefore, in this chapter, two different methods are proposed that exploit sparse classifier to perform AL for HSI. The first method uses only a single spectral feature, while the second method uses a multifeature concept to define the query function. These AL query functions include uncertainty and diversity criteria, both of which are defined by exploiting the SRC in kernel space, known as kernel sparse representation classifier (KSRC). The main rationale of the proposed approach is to define an effective AL criterion for kernel sparse representation classifier. This is important to merge the robustness of this classifier in the analysis of hyperspectral data with the capability to perform the learning phase with a minimum number of training samples selected ad-hoc for satisfying the requirements of KSRC. The main contributions of our methods are: (i) it proposed a robust uncertainty criterion by exploiting KSRC; (ii) it also proposed a novel diversity criterion by exploiting the dictionary of the KSRC; and (iii) it proposed to exploit multiple spectral-spatial feature sets to define better active learning algorithm.

The rest of the chapter is organized as follows. Section 5.2 presents sparse representation classification in kernel space. Section 5.3 describes the proposed active learning methods in detail. Section 5.4 illustrate the datasets used and shows the experimental results and their analysis. Finally, Section 5.5 provides the conclusion and future directions.

5.2 Sparse representation classifiers in kernel space

For HSI $\mathbf{H} \in \mathbb{R}^{P \times Q \times B}$, the sparse representation classifier strategy involves finding a linear combination of atoms (labelled pixels) for an unknown pixel $y \in \mathbb{R}^{B}$ such that:

$$y = \mathrm{D}\alpha \tag{5.1}$$

where $\mathrm{D} = [\mathrm{D}_1, \mathrm{D}_2, ..., \mathrm{D}_\mathrm{C}]$ is a $B \times N$ dictionary containing atoms from C class, where D_i is a subset of the dictionary containing $N_i = |\mathrm{D}_\mathrm{i}|$ atoms of the ith class; hence $N = \sum_{i=1}^{C} N_i$ and α is a sparse vector whose non-zero entries represent the weights of particular atoms.

5.2.1 Kernel Sparse Representation Classification (KSRC)

The kernel sparse representation classifier performs classification by casting the original SRC problem onto higher dimensional feature space [30]. The kernel function $\Phi : \mathcal{X} \rightarrow \mathcal{F}$ projects a pixel of HSI from its original feature space to kernel space. Thus, the unknown pixel y, the dictionary D can be represented in the kernel space as $\Phi(y)$, $\mathrm{V}' = [\Phi(d_1), \Phi(d_2) \dots \Phi(d_N)]$, respectively; where, $\Phi(d_i)$, $i = 1, 2 \dots N$ represents the atom (labelled sample) in higher dimensional kernel space and let α' be the new sparse vector. Therefore, the sparse representation of y in kernel space becomes:

$$\Phi(y) = V'\alpha' \tag{5.2}$$

KSRC follows a two-step procedure. The first step involves finding α' by solving the following optimization problem using greedy kernel orthogonal matching pursuit (KOMP):

$$\hat{\alpha}' = \arg\min \|\Phi(y) - \mathrm{V}'\alpha'\|_2 \quad \textit{subject to} \ \|\alpha'\|_0 < K \tag{5.3}$$

where, K represents the sparsity level and $\|.\|_2$ is the l2-norm. Then, in the second step, the residue between y and its approximation for each class is calculated. Finally, the class label $\hat{c}$ that provides the minimum residue for y is assigned to it, i.e,

$$f(y) = \|\Phi(y) - \mathrm{V}'_{\mathrm{i}}\hat{\alpha}'_{\mathrm{i}}\|_2 \quad \textit{for } i = 1, 2, \dots, C \tag{5.4}$$

$$\hat{c} = \underset{i=1,2,\dots,C}{\arg\min}\{f(y)\} \tag{5.5}$$

5.2.2 Multifeature Kernel Sparse Representation Classification

For a multifeature approach, let $\psi_1, \psi_2, \ldots, \psi_L$ be the L feature sets, y^{ψ_k} represents the pixel y with ψ_k ($k = 1, 2, \ldots, L$) feature set, and the dictionary $D^{\psi_k} = [D_1^{\psi_k}, D_2^{\psi_k}, \ldots, D_C^{\psi_k}]$ contains all the atoms represented with ψ_k feature set. In kernel space, the dictionary D^{ψ_k} is expressed as $V^{\psi_k} = [\Phi(d_1^{\psi_k}), \Phi(d_2^{\psi_k}), \ldots, \Phi(d_N^{\psi_k})]$.

Our proposed MKSRC also follows the same two-step procedure as KSRC [63]. Step one involves kernel orthogonal matching pursuit (KOMP) to solve the following problem.

$$\hat{\alpha}^{\psi_k} = \arg\min \|\Phi(y^{\psi_k}) - V^{\psi_k}\alpha^{\psi_k}\|_2 \quad subject\ to\ \|\alpha^{\psi_k}\|_0 < K$$

The residue between y^{ψ_k} and its approximation is then added up for each class in the second step. Lastly, the class with the total minimum residue was given to it, i.e,

$$f(y) = \sum_{k=1}^{k=L} \|\Phi(y^{\psi_k}) - V_i^{\psi_k}\hat{\alpha}_i^{\psi_k}\|_2\,, \quad for\ i = 1, 2, \ldots, C$$

$$\hat{c} = \arg\min_{i=1,2,\ldots,C}\{f(y)\} \tag{5.6}$$

In order to consider spatial contextual information, an extended version of KSRC known as kernel joint sparse representation classifier (KJSRC) was proposed in [265]. It assumes that neighbouring pixels of an unknown pixel can be represented by linear combination of the same atoms. Hence, their sparse vectors share the same sparsity pattern but with different coefficients. Similarly, the MKSRC can also be extended by adding contextual information to each unlabelled pixel's meaningful features. The extended model is called Multifeature Kernel Joint Sparse Representation Classification (MKJSRC). For details about KJSRC and MKJSRC, the reader may refer to [265] and [119] respectively.

5.3 Proposed Method

In this section, a detailed description is given of both our proposed methods: KBT-DCBD (Kernel Breaking Tie-Dictionary Correlation Based Diversity) and MKBT-MDCBD (Multifeature Kernel Breaking Tie-Multifeature Dictionary Correlation Based Diversity). Both methods use a query function combining uncertainty and diversity criterion, designed using the kernel sparse representation classifier (KSRC). In each AL iteration, their query functions select the h most informative samples by applying uncertainty followed by diversity criteria. The entire framework of our proposed technique is depicted in Figure 5-1. More details regarding these methods will be presented in the following subsections.

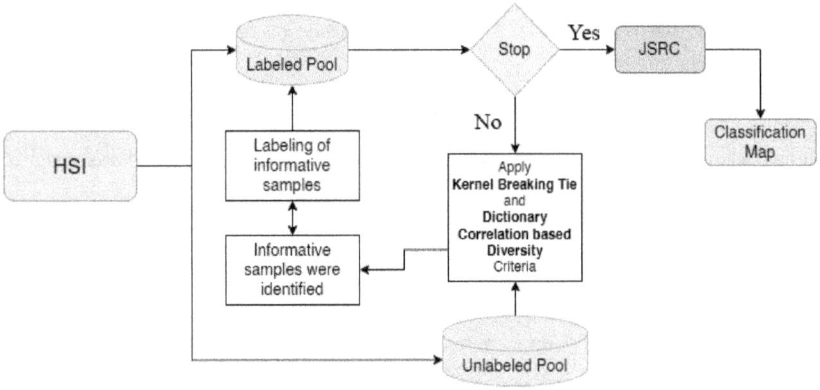

Figure 5-1: Illustration of the framework of the proposed method.

5.3.1 Proposed KBT-DCBD

The query function of KBT-DCBD utilizes a single spectral feature to define an AL for HSI classification. Its uncertainty and diversity criteria are presented below.

5.3.1.1 Proposed Kernel Breaking Tie

In AL, the uncertainty criterion plays a major role in selecting informative samples. As already mentioned, in the literature, most of the AL techniques exploited

SVM classifier to define uncertainty criteria. SRC, a robust and important classifier for HSI classification, has been used for active learning to some extent. However, they have not achieved convincing results as compared to the existing SVM-based AL models. The BT criterion defined in [95] fails to find out appropriate uncertain samples, since the HSI samples that belong to different classes are often highly overlapped. In order to improve the separation between overlapping classes, the kernel sparse representation classifier that projects the samples into a higher dimensional space is a better choice. Accordingly, an uncertainty criterion was introduced, called kernel breaking tie (KBT), that is defined by exploiting the KSRC. Given an unlabelled sample, the reconstruction error for each class is first computed using the dictionary of KSRC. Then the classification confidence, i.e., the difference between lowest and second-lowest reconstruction errors, is used to define the uncertainty level of the sample. The classification confidence $E_{kbt}(y)$ for a sample y in the unlabelled pool $\mathrm{U^P}$ is computed as follows:

$$\iota_1 = \arg\min_{i=1,2,\ldots,C}\{f(y)\}, \qquad \iota_2 = \arg\min_{i=1,2,\ldots,C,\; i\neq l_1}\{f(y)\}$$

$$E_{kbt}(y) = f_{\iota_2}(y) - f_{\iota_1}(y) \tag{5.7}$$

Lower values of $E_{kbt}(y)$ imply that the sample y lies in the boundary region between two classes and is more uncertain. Higher values of $E_{kbt}(y)$ imply that the sample y is less uncertain. The proposed technique selects the batch of uncertain samples from $\mathrm{U^P}$ which have the lowest classification confidence as computed in (5.7).

5.3.1.2 Proposed Dictionary Correlation Based Diversity

In batch mode AL, high redundancy in uncertain samples affects informative sample selection. To mitigate this, a common strategy in the literature involves a two-step approach for each iteration. Initially an uncertainty criterion is applied to select m uncertain samples (may have redundancy) from $\mathrm{U^P}$. Then a diversity criterion is utilized to select a smaller subset of h informative (i.e., both uncertain and non-redundant) samples from these m candidates for labelling. In the literature, there is a large number of diversity criteria such as closest support vector, clustering based diversity, angle based diversity, etc.[47]. We propose, a new diversity criterion called dictionary correlation based diversity (DCBD) by exploiting the dictionary of kernel sparse representation classifier. The DCBD selects samples that have minimum redundancy with the dictionary by measuring the correlation between uncertain samples and the atoms in the dictionary.

Our AL technique first selects m samples $\mathrm{U}^{\mathrm{P}}_{\mathrm{m}} = [y_1, y_2, \ldots y_m]$ from U^{P} using the proposed uncertainty criterion. Then a first order sequential search is performed that selects one sample at a time from $\mathrm{U}^{\mathrm{P}}_{\mathrm{m}}$, having minimum redundancy with the atoms in the dictionary of KSRC. It selects $h(h < m)$ samples from the m uncertain samples. Let $\mathrm{V}' = [\Phi(d_1), \Phi(d_2) \ldots \Phi(d_r)]$ be the initial dictionary of KSRC. For each sample, $y_i \in \mathrm{U}^{\mathrm{P}}_{\mathrm{m}}$ the correlation values between $\Phi(y)$ and all the atoms in V' are computed. Let $< \mathrm{V}', \Phi(y) >$ be the vector that stores m correlation values computed between $\Phi(y)$ and r atoms in V'. We define a function $R(y) = max\{< \mathrm{V}', \Phi(y) >\}$ that takes the maximum correlation value from the vector $< \mathrm{V}', \Phi(y) >$ to measure the redundancy of $\Phi(y)$ in the dictionary V'. High values of $R(y)$ imply that the sample $\Phi(y)$ will be a redundant atom in V'. Thus, in the proposed technique, the sample $y_q \in [y_1, y_2, \ldots y_m]$ that has the least redundancy with the atoms in V' is selected as follows:

$$y_q = \underset{y_1, y_2, \ldots, y_m}{\arg\min} \{R(y_1), R(y_2), \ldots, R(y_m)\} \tag{5.8}$$

After assigning an appropriate label for y_q, the dictionary of KSRC and $\mathrm{U}^{\mathrm{P}}_{\mathrm{m}}$ are updated as $\mathrm{V}' = \mathrm{V}' \cup \{\Phi(y_q)\}$ and $\mathrm{U}^{\mathrm{P}}_{\mathrm{m}} = \mathrm{U}^{\mathrm{P}}_{\mathrm{m}} - \{y_q\}$. The above sequential search is repeated for h times to add h atoms into the dictionary of KSRC with minimum redundancy.

The whole process of the selection of h uncertain and diverse samples for updating the dictionary is repeated until the stopping criterion is met. Finally, the obtained dictionary is used by KJSRC for classification. Algorithm 5 summarizes the proposed AL framework with KBT uncertainty criterion and DCBD diverse criterion. The main theoretical motivation of the proposed technique is that uncertainty and diversity criteria are designed in the kernel sparse representation and not in spaces different from those in which KSRC works. In this way, it is possible to optimize the selection of samples that are the most uncertain and the most diverse in the considered kernel sparse representation space used by the classifier.

Algorithm 5 Proposed AL Method using KBT-DCBD

Let $\mathrm{V}' = [\Phi(d_1), \Phi(d_1), \ldots, \Phi(d_r)]$ be the initial dictionary of KSRC

repeat:

For each $y_i \in \mathrm{U}^{\mathrm{P}}$, compute classification confidence $E_{kbt}(y_i)$ using (5.7)

Select the m uncertain samples $\mathrm{U}^{\mathrm{P}}_{\mathrm{m}}$ from U^{P} that have the lowest classification confidence.

$p = m$

/* To select h informative samples */

for q=1 to h **do**

  for j=1 to p **do**

    Compute Correlation Vector $< \mathrm{V}', \Phi(y_i) >$

    $R(y_j) = max\{< \mathrm{V}, \Phi(y_j) >\}$

  end for

$$y_q = \underset{y_1, y_2, \ldots, y_m}{\arg\min} \{R(y_1), R(y_2), \ldots, R(y_m)\}$$

  Assign appropriate class label to y_q with the help of supervisor.

  Update:

$$\mathrm{V}' = \mathrm{V}' \cup \Phi(y_q)$$
$$\mathrm{U}^{\mathrm{P}}_{\mathrm{m}} = \mathrm{U}^{\mathrm{P}}_{\mathrm{m}} - \{y_q\}$$
$$\mathrm{U}^{\mathrm{P}} = \mathrm{U}^{\mathrm{P}} - \{y_q\}$$

  $p = p - 1$

end for

until stopping criterion is met.

5.3.2 Proposed MKBT-MDCBD

Recently, multifeature approach provides encouraging results for HSI classification [119]. This approach, first, generates multiple feature sets having different perspectives. Then the discriminating power of these feature sets are combined to enhance the separability between classes of HSI. Motivating from it, our second method proposed a novel query function of AL by exploiting the concept of multifeature approach. In this work, both of the above criteria used in KBT-DCBD are further improved by introducing the multifeature concept. We define a multifeature KBT (MKBT) uncertainty criterion and a multifeature DCBD (MDCBD) criterion by modifying the existing KBT and DCBD, respectively. The proposed MKBT and MDCBD criteria are defined by exploiting multiple spectral-spatial feature sets, each having different discriminating power. As a result, our proposed query function is capable of selecting better informative samples than the existing techniques. We described the proposed uncertainty criterion, MKBT and diversity criterion, MDCBD below.

5.3.2.1 Proposed Multifeature Kernel Breaking Tie

In the previous method, the KBT exploited the KSRC to enhance separation between samples. Although it outperformed many state-of-the-art methods, it uses only a single kind of feature. Therefore, to enhance this criterion further, we proposed a Multifeature Kernel Breaking Tie (MKBT), which uses complementary information from multiple spectral-spatial feature sets. This increases the discriminative power of the uncertainty criterion, resulting in the selection of better uncertain samples. The reconstruction error for each class was computed for each unlabelled sample with multiple features using their respective dictionaries. The classification confidence, which is the difference between the lowest and second-lowest approximation errors, was then computed and summarized. This revealed the amount of uncertainty for each sample, with smaller numbers indicating that the samples are extremely uncertain, and vice versa. For a sample y_i in the unlabelled pool $\mathrm{U^P}$, the following formula is used to calculate its classification confidence $E_{mkbt}(y_i)$:

$$\iota_1 = \arg\min_{i=1,2,\ldots,C}\{f(y^{\psi_k})\}, \qquad \iota_2 = \arg\min_{i=1,2,\ldots,C,\ i\neq l_1}\{f(y^{\psi_k})\}$$

$$E_{kbt}(y^{\psi_k}) = f_{\iota_2}(y^{\psi_k}) - f_{\iota_1}(y^{\psi_k})$$

$$E_{mkbt}(y) = \sum_{k=1}^{k=L} E_{kbt}(y^{\psi_k}) \tag{5.9}$$

5.3.2.2 Proposed Multifeature Dictionary Correlation Based Diversity

The samples selected by the above multifeature uncertainty criterion may contain similar information, which increase the redundancy on the dictionary. Following the steps above, multifeature sets were incorporated into the DCBD method to create a new criterion that handle this problem. It uses a composite kernel that establishes stronger correlation between the uncertain samples and the dictionary in multifeature kernel space. Using this correlation, their total redundancy was calculated and a subset of sample with the least total redundancy were labelled and added to the dictionaries.

Given, $\mathrm{V}^{\psi_k} = [\Phi(d_1^{\psi_k}), \Phi(d_2^{\psi_k}) \ldots \Phi(d_r^{\psi_k})]$ be the initial dictionary of the ψ_k feature set. Let $\mathrm{U^P_m} = [y_1, y_2, \ldots y_m]$ denote the set of m uncertain samples drawn from unlabelled pool using the proposed MKBT. The first step is calculating the correlation coefficients between each uncertain feature $\Phi(y^{\psi_k})$ and all the atoms in V^{ψ_k} for each sample y. Then, the total correlation is computed and stored in Γ as, $\Gamma = \sum_{k=1}^{k=L} < \Phi(y^{\psi_k}), \mathrm{V}^{\psi_k} >$. Next, in order to calculate the total degree of redundancy of $\Phi(y_i)$, a function $R(y_i) = max\{\Gamma\}$ is used that extracts the maximum correlation value from the vector Γ. The sample $y_q \in [y_1, y_2, \ldots y_m]$ with the lowest values of $R(y_i)$ signifies that it is non-redundant sample and will be selected as follows:

$$y_q = \underset{y_1, y_2, \ldots, y_m}{\arg\min} \{R(y_1), R(y_2), \ldots, R(y_m)\} \tag{5.10}$$

The sample y_q is then assigned a label and the dictionaries of MKSRC V^{ψ_k} and $\mathrm{U}^{\mathrm{P}}_{\mathrm{m}}$ are updated as $\mathrm{V}^{\psi_k} = \mathrm{V}^{\psi_k} \cup \{\Phi(y_q^{\psi_k})\}$ and $\mathrm{U}^{\mathrm{P}}_{\mathrm{m}} = \mathrm{U}^{\mathrm{P}}_{\mathrm{m}} - \{y_q\}$. The proposed diversity criterion continues until h atoms are included in the dictionaries. The process is repeated until the stopping condition. At the end, the obtained dictionary is used for classification.

Algorithm 6 Proposed AL Method using MKBT-MDCBD

Input: Hyperspectral Image **H**; unlabelled pool U^P;Dictionaries D^{ψ_k}; sparsity level K

Let $\mathrm{V}^{\psi_k} = [\Phi(d_1^{\psi_k}), \Phi(d_1^{\psi_k}), \ldots, \Phi(d_r^{\psi_k})]$ be the MKSRC first dictionary.
repeat:
For all $y_i \in \mathrm{U}^{\mathrm{P}}$, calculate $E_{mkbt}(y_i)$ using (5.9)
Select the m uncertain samples $\mathrm{U}^{\mathrm{P}}_{\mathrm{m}}$ having the lowest classification confidence from U^{P}.
$p = m$
/* Selecting the h non-redundant (informative) samples */
for q=1 to h **do**
    for j=1 to p **do**
        Calculate $\Gamma = \sum_{k=1}^{k=L} < \Phi(y_j^{\psi_k}), \mathrm{V}^{\psi_k} >$.
        $R(y_j) = max\{\Gamma\}$
    end for
    Compute y_q using (5.10)
    Give correct class label to y_q using the supervisor's help.
    Update:

$$\mathrm{V}^{\psi_k} = \mathrm{V}^{\psi_k} \cup \Phi(y_q^{\psi_k})$$
$$\mathrm{U}^{\mathrm{P}} = \mathrm{U}^{\mathrm{P}} - \{y_q\}$$
$$\mathrm{U}^{\mathrm{P}}_{\mathrm{m}} = \mathrm{U}^{\mathrm{P}}_{\mathrm{m}} - \{y_q\}$$

    $p = p - 1$
end for
until stopping condition.

5.4 Experimental Results

This section describes the experimental design and the results acquired by the proposed technique.

5.4.1 Design of Experiments

In order to show the robustness of our proposed methods, three datasets are used for evaluation. The description of each of these datasets is given in Appendix A. Two sets of experiments are conducted for each method, one to show the potentiality of the proposed uncertainty criteria, KBT and MKBT criterion for selecting uncertain samples and the other to show the potentiality of the proposed diversity criteria, DCBD and MDCBD for selecting informative samples.

The first experiment aims to assess the effectiveness of the proposed uncertainty criterion. The KBT and MKBT criterion is compared with several popular state-of-the-art uncertainty criteria like, Marginal Sampling (MS) [148], Multi Class Level Uncertainty (MCLU) [47] Entropy Query-by-Bagging (EQB) [225] and Sparse Representation based BT (SRC-BT) [95]. In the second experiment, to assess the effectiveness of the proposed diversity criterion, the KBT-DCBD and MKBT-MDCBD techniques are compared with three state-of-the-art AL techniques i.e. marginal sampling with the closest support vector (MS-cSV) [225], multi class level uncertainty with kernel kmeans (MCLU-KK) [47] and MCLU-KK with edge gradient (MCLU-KK-EG) [188]. Furthermore, two type of spatial features were considered in addition to the spectral feature in MKBT-MDCBD. These are Extended Morphological Attribute Profile (EMAP) and Differential Morphological Profile (DMP). The detailed parameters for these two features is presented in Table 5.1.

The classification results of the proposed technique did not change significantly by varying the sparsity level K of KSRC and the γ of RBF kernel within the range $[3, 9]$ and $[2^5, 2^8]$, respectively. For the present experiment, the value of K is fixed to 9 for the University of Houston dataset and to 3 for the other datasets. The value of γ is fixed to 2^7 and the level of sparsity for KJSRC is set to 30 for all the datasets.

Table 5.1: Parameters for EMAP and DMP extraction.

Feature	Parameters
EMAP	Base Images : PC1,PC2,PC3,PC4,PC5 Attribute : area Threshold : 10, 25, 50, 80, 120, 150, 200, 290.
DMP	Base Images : PC1, PC2 SE λ : 3, 5, 7, 9, 11, 13, 15, 17.

At the beginning of AL, 3 samples from each class are randomly selected to form the initial training set (dictionary). Subsequently, in each iteration of AL, $h = 5$ samples are selected and assigned to their appropriate labels for updating the training set (dictionary). The MS-cSV, MCLU-KK, MCLU-KK-EG, and the KBT-DCBD techniques, first select m uncertain samples, then choose h informative samples from m for labelling. The value of m is set to $3h$ in the experiments. The AL techniques are executed for 30 iterations, resulting in 198, 189, and 195 samples in the training set (dictionary) for Indian Pines, Kennedy Space Center, and University of Houston 2013 datasets, respectively. The rest of the samples in U (i.e., 10051, 4838, and 14839 samples for Indian Pines, Kennedy Space Center, and University of Houston 2013 datasets) are used for testing. Experiments are performed in 5 runs to reduce random effects on the results.

All experiments were conducted within a 64-bit Matlab environment, utilizing a desktop computer equipped with a 64-bit operating system, an Intel(R) Core(TM) i5 8400 CPU with a clock speed of 2.80GHz, and 16 GB of random-access memory (RAM).

5.4.2 Results

In this section, we first analyse the results of KBT-DCBD against other state-of-the-art methods and then analyse the results of its multifeature approach MKBT-MDCBD.

In this section, Table 5.2 show the results of the first experiment using KBT

Table 5.2: Average overall accuracy ($\overline{OA}$) and standard deviation (sd) obtained by the MS [148], MCLU [225], EQB[225], SRC-BT [95], Proposed KBT and Proposed MKBT for Indian Pines, KSC and University of Houston 2013 datasets

Indian Pines								
Method	$N = 83$		$N = 123$		$N = 163$		$N = 198$	
	$\overline{OA}$	sd	$\overline{OA}$	sd	$\overline{OA}$	sd	$\overline{OA}$	sd
MS	54.07	± 3.12	59.99	± 2.46	64.13	± 3.05	66.86	± 2.57
MCLU	51.66	± 2.74	58.54	± 1.62	63.31	±2.55	66.73	± 2.25
EQB	47.55	± 2.93	54.68	± 1.23	58.30	± 1.32	61.43	± 2.25
SRC-BT	52.78	± 1.51	55.79	± 1.91	57.33	± 1.49	58.45	± 1.40
Proposed KBT	65.51	± 2.33	73.89	± 2.76	76.17	± 1.77	77.75	± 1.49
Proposed MKBT	64.80	± 3.11	77.25	±1.50	82.38	± 0.42	85.78	± 1.57
Kennedy Space Center								
Method	$N = 79$		$N = 119$		$N = 154$		$N = 189$	
	$\overline{OA}$	sd	$\overline{OA}$	sd	$\overline{OA}$	sd	$\overline{OA}$	sd
MS	81.81	± 2.25	86.40	± 1.24	88.06	± 0.86	88.70	± 0.42
MCLU	83.99	± 0.87	86.53	± 1.28	88.76	± 0.54	90.47	± 0.94
EQB	80.94	± 1.70	85.85	± 1.25	87.73	± 0.99	89.35	± 0.92
SRC-BT	65.29	± 2.82	68.12	±4.01	69.65	± 4.49	72.85	± 2.66
Proposed KBT	85.27	± 2.79	91.76	± 1.59	93.85	± 0.98	94.17	± 0.90
Proposed MKBT	83.62	± 3.02	90.05	± 4.14	94.70	± 2.06	97.65	± 1.14
University of Houston 2013								
Method	$N = 80$		$N = 135$		$N = 160$		$N = 195$	
	$\overline{OA}$	sd	$\overline{OA}$	sd	$\overline{OA}$	sd	$\overline{OA}$	sd
MS	72.82	± 3.77	77.63	± 2.13	80.92	± 1.04	82.92	± 0.53
MCLU	71.81	± 1.73	78.49	± 2.22	82.18	± 2.24	84.15	± 2.16
EQB	68.03	± 3.02	73.10	± 1.88	76.63	± 1.81	79.36	± 2.56
SRC-BT	66.86	± 1.23	69.86	± 0.94	73.57	± 1.49	75.31	± 1.65
Proposed KBT	74.23	± 1.73	78.55	± 1.14	82.57	± 1.21	83.97	± 1.54
Proposed MKBT	76.23	± 2.54	79.87	± 2.44	83.33	± 1.67	85.53	± 1.50

Table 5.3: Computational time in seconds taken by the MS-cSV, MCLU-KK, MCLU-KK-EG, SRC-BT, KBT and KBT-DCBD for different datasets.

Dataset	**MS-cSV**	**MCLU-KK**	**MCLU-KK-EG**	**SRC-BT**	**KBT**	**KBT-DCBD**	**MKBT-MDCBD**
IP	395.75	131.08	138.98	398.13	174.99	175.92	457.11
KSC	190.03	49.64	51.08	386.12	73.93	74.33	181.06
UH	491.17	134.98	135.84	521.56	242.87	243.92	603.78

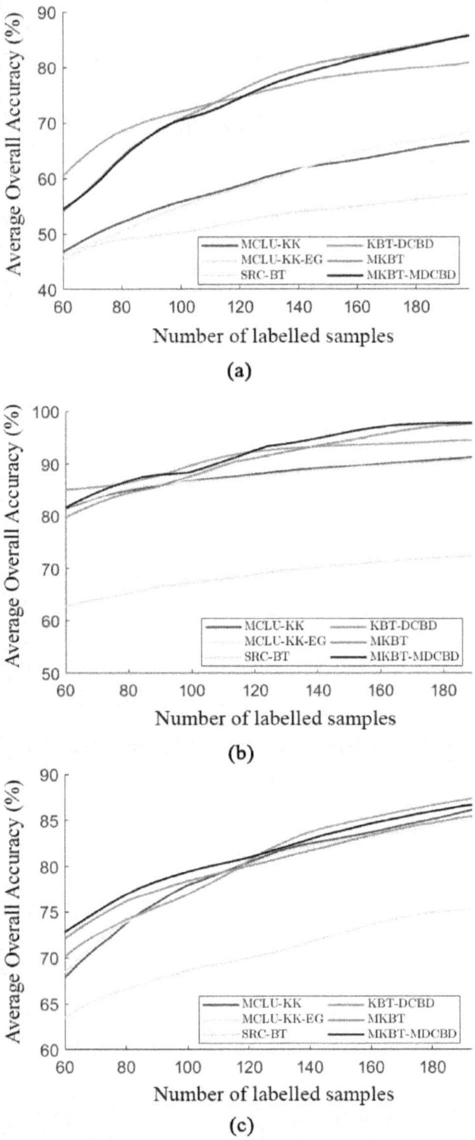

Figure 5-2: Overall Average Accuracy ($\overline{OA}$) versus the number of labelled samples of different AL methods for a) Indian Pines, b) KSC, c) University of Houston 2013 datasets

and MKBT respectively obtained at different iteration of AL for Indian Pines, KSC and University of Houston 2013. It provides the average overall accuracy ($\overline{OA}$) and the standard deviation (sd) for all techniques under varying numbers of labelled samples N. The table illustrates that the proposed uncertainty criterion (i.e., KBT) outperforms many popular state-of-the-art uncertainty criteria that exist in the AL literature for all the datasets. For the Indian Pines dataset, the proposed criterion provides at least 10% higher average overall accuracy ($\overline{OA}$) than the best literature criterion (i.e., MS). Similarly, for KSC dataset, the KBT provides nearly 4% higher $\overline{OA}$ than the best literature criterion. For the University of Houston 2013 dataset, the proposed criterion provides similar results as provided by the best literature criterion (i.e., MCLU). However, the second proposed multifeature criterion MKBT have significantly surpassed the KBT and outperform other state-of-the-art uncertainty criteria as well. For Indian Pines, it produces an $\overline{OA}$ of 85.78%, which is 8% higher than our proposed KBT. Similarly, for KSC and Houston dataset, the MKBT produce a classification accuracy $\overline{OA}$ of 97.65% and 85.53 % respectively, which is significantly higher compared to other considered techniques. Thus, the results show the potentiality of the proposed KBT and MKBT criteria to select better uncertain samples.

The results of the second experiment for Indian Pines, KSC and Houston 2013 dataset are shown in Figure 5-2. From these figures, one can see that our proposed KBT-DCBD and MKBT-MDCBD provides significantly better results than many other state-of-the-art methods. Note that only at the beginning, the MKBT-MDCBD failed to provide better results than KBT-DCBD. This is because at the initial iterations of AL, the decision function of the classifier may be passed through completely wrong regions in the feature space. So, the diverse samples selected by MDCBD may not be useful to provide additional information to the classifier. For the Indian Pines dataset, our KBT-DCBD technique provides an $\overline{OA}$ of 80.91% by labelling only 198 samples, whereas with the same number of labelled samples, the best literature method (i.e., the MCLU-KK-EG) provides only 68.32%. For KSC dataset, our technique provides an $\overline{OA}$ of 94.48% by labelling only 189 samples, whereas the best literature method (i.e., the MCLU-

KK) obtains 91.28%. Similarly, for the University of Houston 2013 dataset the proposed KBT-DCBD technique provides an $\overline{OA}$ of 87.48%, whereas the best literature method MCLU-KK provides 86.31% of $\overline{OA}$. Regarding the second proposed method, MKBT-MDCBD, the results from the Figure 5-2 shows that the accuracy was further improved by it. It produces an $\overline{OA}$ of 85.69% for Indian Pines dataset and $\overline{OA}$ of 97.78% for KSC dataset, which is higher than all the considered AL techniques. For the University of Houston 2013 dataset, the MKBT-MDCBD produces an $\overline{OA}$ of 86.78% which is comparable to the proposed KBT-DCBD method.

From the results of these experiments, it is observed that the improvements made by both proposed methods are possible because of the sparse representation in kernel space, which is exploited by the proposed technique for designing better uncertainty and diversity criteria. Furthermore, the addition of multiple features into this kernel model to form MKBT-MDCBD has shown that the multiple feature sets provided complementary information for selecting those informative samples that are not only informative from the spectral perspective, but also from spatial perspective. Finally, the computational time required by the different techniques is reported in Table 5.2. As observed in this table, the computational cost of the proposed technique is comparable to that of existing methods in the literature.

5.5 Conclusion

The goal of this research is to develop a novel robust query function to improve the effectiveness of AL in identifying appropriate informative samples to label for the training of a KSRC. The proposed uncertainty and diversity criteria are designed in the kernel sparse representation and not in spaces different from those in which KSRC works, like in other literature methods. So, it is possible to optimize the selection of samples that are the most uncertain and the most diverse in the considered kernel sparse representation space used by the classifier, with the results obtaining a very good trade-off between labelling cost and classification accuracy. The robustness of the proposed methods is validated by using three real benchmark HSI datasets. The proposed method improves the classification accuracy with a reduced number of labelled training data for all the datasets. This is very important and goes in the direction of improving the real-life deployment of an automatic classifier as results in a reduction of the cost for labelling training data with respect to other literature methods. Moreover, the proposed method: i) is based on a simple design; ii) is fast; iii) does not have critical requirements on memory; and iv) exploits a sparse classifier robust to high-dimensional feature spaces.

Chapter 6

Conclusion and future direction

The main purpose of this thesis is to overcome the challenges associated with classifying HSIs. This is accomplished by developing robust methods that exploit sparse representation-based classifiers for effective analysis of HSI. To achieve this, four contributions are presented in this thesis. In this chapter, a summarization of each contribution is given, along with their limitations and future works.

6.1 Contribution 1 : A component adaptive sparse representation classification

The existing techniques predominantly utilize fixed-size windows or superpixels to consider spatial contextual information of the pixel. However, the inability to simultaneously consider the correlated information at different scales and appropriate spatial neighbourhoods limits their performance. In this thesis, a novel method is proposed that constructs modified max-tree and min-tree to represent the connected components of the image for better modelling of the spatial contextual information. The proposed method then exploit these connected components to define adaptive multiscale windows that determine the appropriate spatial neighbourhoods of the pixels in HSI. Finally, the multiscale spatial neighbourhoods of the pixels are fed into a sparse classification model to classify the HSI.

The experimental results demonstrate that in contrast to the state-of-the-art methods, the proposed technique always provided good results irrespective of the datasets considered. Even on challenging standard training and test sets from the remote sensing community, the proposed technique provides significantly higher accuracy than the best method in the literature.

6.1.1 Limitations and future works

1. The filter images generated by the proposed technique are dependent upon the user defined thresholds. The user must have some prior information regarding the nature of HSI. Although this is not a critical parameter, for further improvement we plan to use optimization techniques such as swarm optimization to find out the optimal thresholds.

2. In this research, the proposed technique exploited only *area* attribute to define component adaptive spatial windows. Exploitation of other attributes will be an interesting future development of this work.

6.2 Contribution 2: A novel dictionary learning method for HSI Classification

Several dictionary learning techniques have effectively improved the sparse representation model's ability to classify the HSI. However, their level of effectiveness is dependent on the discriminative power of the spectral or spectral-spatial information used to learn the dictionary. In this thesis, to learn compact, qualitative, and comprehensive dictionaries, each pixel is represented by a feature set extracted by considering its relevant spatial neighbourhood. Note that in contrast to the first approach, a simple and computationally efficient technique is proposed to define each pixel's appropriate spatial neighbourhoods. The method first uses superpixels and a fixed window to identify the appropriate spatial neighbourhoods of the pixel. Then, considering each spatial neighbourhood of the pixel, SVD is used to extract the context-sensitive spectral features (CSSF) of it. Thus, for a pixel, multiple CSSFs are extracted by considering its spatial neighbourhoods at different scales. Then, for each CSSF, a dictionary is learned by adopting the DKSVD dictionary learning algorithm. Finally, the classification results provided by the individual dictionary are ensembles to predict the final result.

The effectiveness of the proposed technique has been rigorously evaluated through a comparative analysis with other state-of-the-art techniques across three HSI datasets. The experimental results consistently demonstrate that, in contrast to the state-of-the-art methods, the proposed technique yielded the best and most consistent performance across all considered datasets.

6.2.1 Limitations and future works

1. One limitation of the proposed method is that the multiscale CSSF cannot be fused together to be used as a single feature set for classification as the number of features in each CSSF is very high (i.e. it is equal to the number of HSI bands). Therefore, developing a method to overcome this limitation could be a promising area for future research.

2. Also as a future work, the method will be tested with other remote sensing datasets such as multispectral, Synthetic Aperture Radar (SAR), Polarimetric SAR etc.

6.3 Contribution 3: A novel spectral-spatial feature set for HSI classification

The extraction of robust spectral-spatial features remains a challenging research issue due to the low interclass and high intraclass variability of HSI. In this thesis, we present a novel method designed to address this challenge by extracting effective spectral-spatial features from HSI pixels. Note that in contrast to the first and second methods, here multiple fixed window of increasing size are used to define spatial neighbourhoods of the pixel. The method first reduces the dimensionality of the HSI by applying principal component analysis (PCA). Then it exploits SVD to obtain the rank-1 approximation of the pixels inside a fixed-size window. The features associated to the center pixel of the window, which are called rank-1 spectral-spatial features (RSSF) are then used to represent the pixel. Since a single window may not define the appropriate spatial neighbourhood of the center pixel, multiple windows of increasing size are considered, resulting in the generation of multiple RSSFs. These RSSFs are stacked together to form a Multiscale RSSF (MRSSF). Finally, the pixels represented with their MRSSF are fed into a sparse classification model to classify the HSI.

The proposed method's effectiveness has been compared with seven state-of-the art feature sets and five deep learning methods using four datasets. The experimental results show that the proposed technique always provided good and consistent results.

6.3.1 Limitations and future works

1. In this proposed method, simple fixed-size windows were used to capture the spatial contextual information of pixels. However, research on developing smart ways to capture this information can also be done to improve the classification performance.

6.4 Contribution 4: Active learning criteria by exploiting KSRC

Sparse representation classifier (SRC) has proven to be a robust classifier and has successfully been applied to HSI classification. However, despite recent significant advancements, it has been found that SRC is rarely applied in the context of active learning. Therefore, the aim of this contribution is to develop a novel robust query functions based on SRC, that will improve AL's efficiency in selecting informative samples for labelling. To this end, two query functions KBT-DCBD and MKBT-MDCBD were developed to perform AL for HSI using the kernel sparse representation classifier (KSRC). The first one uses only a single spectral feature, while the second one uses multiple set of features. Both functions incorporate uncertainty and diversity criteria specifically designed for KSRC's kernel space. This ensures that selected samples are both uncertain and diverse within the

KSRC's representation space, leading to a balance between labelling cost and classification accuracy.

The robustness of the proposed methods is validated by using three real benchmark HSI datasets. And it was found that both the proposed methods produces good classification accuracy with a reduced number of labelled training data. But between the two, MKBT-MDCBD's use of multiple feature sets results in a more refined uncertainty and diversity criteria, leading to even better classification performance.

6.4.1 Limitations and future works

1. The KSRC, which is used to identify uncertain samples, can be computationally slow for very large datasets. This can increase the overall processing time of the proposed methods. To address this, parallelization techniques could be explored to speed up the computations.

2. The multiple feature sets used to extract informative samples were simply assumed to be of equal importance, but in a real scenario, some feature will offer more important information than the others. Therefore, a mechanism that assigns more weight to an important feature can be devised to improve the decision-making process.

Overall, the proposed methods in this thesis consistently achieve strong performance across four widely used hyperspectral datasets that differ significantly in both spatial and spectral resolution. Across all datasets, the proposed techniques maintain high overall accuracy and strong class-wise performance, indicating good generalization to varying pixel sizes, spatial textures, and scene complexities. The methods presented in Chapters 2 and 3, including component-adaptive sparse representation and multiscale context-sensitive spectral feature extraction, demonstrate robustness to variations in spatial granularity by effectively capturing both local and multiscale neighborhood information. Furthermore, the rank-1 multiscale spectral–spatial features introduced in Chapter 4 exhibit stable performance despite variations in the number of available spectral bands, highlighting the ability of the proposed approach to jointly exploit spectral redundancy and spatial structure. Collectively, these results confirm that the proposed methods deliver accurate and reliable performance irrespective of the dataset used, and suggest that the approach can be extended to other hyperspectral datasets, including satellite-based imagery such as PRISMA and EnMAP.

From a computational perspective, the proposed methods achieve manageable execution times on standard benchmark datasets, even when incorporating multiscale spatial neighborhoods and sparse representation techniques. While the computational cost may increase when applied to significantly larger hyperspectral scenes, this limitation can be effectively addressed through parallel processing strategies and GPU acceleration, enabling scalability to large-scale datasets.

www.ingramcontent.com/pod-product-compliance
Lightning Source LLC
LaVergne TN
LVHW010731061126
851857LV00014B/1427
* 9 7 8 1 9 6 2 1 1 6 7 3 2 *